Options Trading

FOR

DUMMIES®

OPTIONETICS® CUSTOM EDITION

by Traci Cumbay

BICENTENNIAL
1807
WILEY
2007
BICENTENNIAL

Wiley Publishing, Inc.

Options Trading For Dummies®, Optionetics® Custom Edition

Published by
Wiley Publishing, Inc.
111 River Street
Hoboken, NJ 07030-5774
www.wiley.com

For general information on our other products and services or to obtain technical support, please contact our Customer Care Department within the U.S. at 800-762-2974, outside the U.S. at 317-572-3993, or fax 317-572-4002.

Wiley also publishes its books in a variety of electronic formats. Some content that appears in print may not be available in electronic books.

ISBN: 978-0-470-12682-0

Manufactured in the United States of America

10 9 8 7 6 5 4 3 2 1

1O/SS/RS/QW/IN

WILEY

Table of Contents

Publisher's Acknowledgments

We're proud of this book; please send us your comments through our online registration form located at www.dummies.com/register/. For details about how to create a For Dummies book for your company or organization, please contact dummiesrights &licenses@wiley.com.

Some of the people who helped bring this book to market include the following:

Acquisitions, Editorial, and Media Development

Project Editor: Janet Sims

Business Development Representative: Karen Hattan

Editorial Manager: Rev Mengle

Composition Services

Project Coordinator: Kristie Rees

Layout and Graphics: Brooke Graczyk, Denny Hager, Shane Johnson, Alicia B. South, Julie Trippetti

Proofreaders: Sossity R. Smith

Indexer: Lynnzee Elze

Publishing and Editorial for Technology Dummies

    Richard Swadley, Vice President and Executive Group Publisher

    Andy Cummings, Vice President and Publisher

    Mary C. Corder, Editorial Director

Publishing for Consumer Dummies

    Diane Graves Steele, Vice President and Publisher

    Joyce Pepple, Acquisitions Director

Composition Services

    Gerry Fahey, Vice President of Production Services

    Debbie Stailey, Director of Composition Services

Optionetics, Inc. Acknowledgments

Special thanks to Clare White, CMS, and Maya Markowitz for their hard work in creating an excellent options education tool.

Introduction

● ●

*A*n option is the world's most versatile trading instrument. It enables traders to capitalize on the bullish or bearish moves of an underlying market — usually with much less initial capital than buying stocks outright.

Imagine making 200%, 300%, or even 800% returns in a matter of days. With options, you can. Option trades commonly generate three times more profit than comparable stock trades. And because options cost much less than the underlying stocks themselves, risk is inherently limited. In other words, trading options just makes sense.

Options can seem like a daunting subject, but it's not rocket science. Ordinary people profit from using options in their everyday trading.

Learning to trade is a cumulative process where experience and knowledge go hand-in-hand. The integration of options into your trading approach is a vital key to helping you become a successful trader.

About This Book

This book provides valuable insight for traders of all levels — and even people new to the markets — who are interested in learning more about the power of options and how to trade them for profit. Consider it a comprehensive overview of Optionetics' broad range of high-reward, low-risk, low-stress trading strategies.

Trading options comes with a unique set of instructions that is very different from trading stocks, bonds, or commodities. For long-term profits, option traders need to develop a distinctive group of skills and adopt a new way of thinking about the markets. By following fundamental risk management guidelines and investment strategies, trading options can be extremely lucrative and worthwhile, as this handy guide demonstrates.

Here's what you find in *Options Trading For Dummies*:

Part 1: Fundamentals of Options

This part covers all the basics about trading options. Chapter 1 introduces you to the bare-bones facts about options — what they are and why they make sense for traders. Chapter 2 tells you about four kinds of trades you can make with options and how each one stacks up. Of course, trying to trade without having a hold on option quotes is kind of like attempting to draw without a pencil. So Chapter 3 translates the language of option quotes into plain English. What makes an option worth one amount on Tuesday and another on Saturday? Chapter 4 explains the factors that determine an option's price.

Part 11: Options Trading Strategies

This part takes you a little deeper into understanding options. How a stock behaves can tell you a lot about what you can expect from a particular option. Chapter 5 explains what these factors mean for traders. Chapter 6 gives you some advanced techniques for figuring out how risky a particular trade might be. Then comes the moment you've been waiting for: Chapter 7 gives you information about placing your trade effectively and fills you in on how to make trading as low-stress as possible.

Part 111: The Part of Tens

This part has two "top ten" lists to help you get started in options trading. Chapter 8 offers some advice and a handy checklist for choosing a broker. For traders of any level, Optionetics provides all kinds of valuable resources. Chapter 9 highlights ten of them.

Appendix: A Trader's Glossary

Not familiar with a term you came across in Chapter 2? Stumped by a phrase in Chapter 5? Turn here to get its meaning.

Who Should Read This Book?

Becoming a successful options trader involves stepping back and evaluating the motivating factors behind your actions. What is your rationale for wanting to trade? To generate extra cash? To spend more time with your family and friends? To retire early? To travel?

Whatever your personal financial goals, infusing your long-term investments with options may be just the trick to increase your income or savings, protect against market downturns and provide the leverage you need to make significant earnings.

If you work for a company that offers its employees stock options, you especially need to understand how options work in order to make the best of your assets.

If you're interested in attaining true financial freedom and living life on *your* terms, then you'll find this book an extremely valuable resource.

Icons Used in This Book

Throughout this book, I occasionally use icons to call attention to material worth noting in a special way. Here's a description of each:

Points that are critical to your understanding of option trading are highlighted by this icon.

Information that helps you trade more effectively or may save you time or money is accompanied by this icon.

Unless you're planning a career as a trader, the inside information marked by this icon may not turn your crank. Feel free to skip it.

We steer you away from trading pitfalls with this icon.

Where To Go from Here

This book concentrates on lower-risk strategies, although it does briefly look at a couple of the higher risk strategies (short calls and puts) to put things in perspective. Keep in mind that your best tactic is to master one technique before moving on to another.

You can create many different strategies with different risk profiles ranging from low to high risk. Work with the techniques to find the ones that are most suitable to your style and objectives.

Part I

Fundamentals of Options

Defining your investment risk with the:
TOAST RETRIEVING RISK TOLERANCE TEST

LOW RISK | Waits for toast to pop up even though it's burning.

MODERATE RISK | Goes after toast with wooden toast prongs.

HIGH RISK | Goes after toast with all metal butter knife.

ULTRA HIGH RISK | Goes after toast with metal butter knife wearing a wet swim suit and a stainless steel colander on head.

In this part . . .

This part of the book explains the basics of stock options: how they work and how trading in options may just help you make a fortune — or at least see higher returns through both "bullish" and "bearish" markets. This part introduces the types of option trades you can make and explains the pros and cons of each "position." You also find out how to read an option quote and how to place an option "put" or "call" with your broker. When you have these terms and concepts under your belt, you're well on your way to making your first trade in the wide world of options.

Chapter 1

Trader, Meet Options

. . . .

In This Chapter

▶ What options are made of, why they're a good bet

▶ Deconstructing options

▶ Looking into an options trade

. . . .

*I*n essence, an option is the right, but not the obligation, to do something. Options provide choices for how you may wish to proceed, not just in trading, but in the situations you encounter in everyday life.

Options play a similar role in trading. In that world, an *option* is a contract between two parties — a buyer and a seller — that conveys the right but not the obligation to buy or sell something, usually shares of stock.

Here are a few of the benefits of investing in options:

✔ You can buy options for less than 10% of a stock's value.

✔ Options can significantly increase in value when the stocks move as little as 5%.

✔ You can trade options short-term (30 to 90 days), longer term (up to 3 years), or anywhere in between.

✔ Options enable you to make money when stock values decrease.

Another great advantage of trading options is that you can turn a tidy profit in up, down, and sideways markets. Can your traditional mutual fund do that? In fact, trading options allows you to make money *regardless of market direction*. By buying put options, you can achieve leveraged gains with limited dollar risk when a stock price declines; and by purchasing call options, you can make leveraged gains on a stock price upsurge. You can also use specific trading strategies that let you profit in range-bound markets.

Not all stocks have options. Check out the Optionetics Web site (www.optionetics.com) to determine whether a stock has options.

Why Trade Options?

Options provide amazing versatility and a welcome relief from the uncertainties of traditional investing practices. You can use them in a variety of ways to profit from a rise or fall in the underlying market, as well as to increase your leverage by controlling the shares of a specific stock without tying up a large amount of capital.

Options have a wide variety of uses, including the following applications:

- ✔ Options enable you to buy a stock at a lower price by exercising an in-the-money call option. Turn to Chapter 4 to find out more about in-the-money call options.

- ✔ Options enable you to sell a stock at a higher price by exercising an in-the-money put option. (See Chapter 4.)

- ✔ Options create additional income against a long or short stock position. Chapter 2 tells you more about going long or short.

- ✔ Options can be combined to create strategies that offer limited risk approaches to taking advantage of bullish, bearish, and sideways markets. Check out Chapters 3 and 6 to find out more about risk.

- ✔ Specific option strategies can profit from a move in the price of the underlying asset regardless of market direction. Find out more about gauging the market in Chapter 5.

Buying an option offers limited risk and unlimited profit potentials. In contrast, selling an option (also known as writing an option) comes with an obligation to complete the trade if the party who buys it chooses to exercise the option. Selling an option therefore presents the writer with limited profit potential and significant risk, unless the position is hedged in some manner.

Options are the perfect trading instrument for leveraging your capital and hedging your portfolio against risk. They act to protect your investments just as buying insurance would for your car or home. Many of us could have probably done a better job "insuring" our portfolio against losses. But only hindsight is 20/20. To be successful in today's markets, you need to evaluate your current positions to see what you can do to be successful as you move forward. Finally, understanding the ins and outs of assignment and how it works in real-world trading is vital to becoming a successful options trader.

Anatomy of an Option

Several variables distinguish an individual option from every other available option. Each time you enter a trade using options; these five terms define the parameters of your trade. Understanding these factors and what they mean for each trade maximizes your chances of success.

Option types

Options come in two flavors — calls and puts — depending on whether you contract for the right to buy or sell.

Call options

A *call option* gives the buyer the right to buy a fixed number of shares (usually 100) of an underlying stock at a specified price before the option expiration date. Ideally (for the buyer), the price of the underlying stock rises before the call expires. Of course, whoever's selling the call hopes that the price of the underlying stock declines or remains below the call strike price until it expires.

Assume, for example, that Walt Disney Company (DIS) shares have a last sale price of $26. An available standard call option contract would be a DIS January 25 call. Buy this contract and you have the right — but not the obligation — to buy 100 DIS shares for $25 per share at any time before the expiration date in January.

For this right, you pay a premium (the option purchase price) to the writer (seller) of the option. In order to take up this right to buy the DIS shares at the specified price, you have to exercise the option by the last trading day before its expiration day in January.

On the other hand, for this option to exist, someone sold this right. This trader is referred to as a *writer* of the call option. Instead of owning a right, the writer has an obligation; in this case he or she is obliged to deliver 100 DIS shares at $25 per share if you exercise your call option. For accepting this obligation, the writer receives and keeps the option premium regardless of whether you exercise the option or not.

If you exercise the call option, you purchase the shares at the specified exercise (strike) price.

Put options

A *put option* gives the buyer the right to sell a fixed number of shares of an underlying stock at a specified price before the option expiration date. If you're the buyer of a put option, you want the price of the underlying stock to drop before the put expires. And the seller (that is, writer) of the put banks on the price of the underlying stock rising — or at least staying the same — until the put expires.

Here's how it works: Assume Alcoa Inc. (AA) shares have a closing stock price of $28.20 on a given day. This means the last official trade on the exchange for that day occurred at $28.20. An available standard put option contract would be an October AA 30 put. This gives the buyer (taker) the right — but not the obligation — to sell 100 AA shares for $30 per share at any time before the October expiration day.

For this right, the buyer pays a premium (the option purchase price) to the writer of the put option. In order to take up this right to sell the AA shares at the specified price the buyer must exercise the option by the last trading day before the expiration date in October.

The writer of the put option is obliged to buy the AA shares for $30 per share if the option is exercised. Just as with call options, the writer of a put option receives and keeps the option premium whether the option is exercised or not.

If the put option is exercised, the shares are traded at the specified exercise (strike) price.

Underlying security

Options fall into a security category known as *derivatives* because an option value is derived from, or based upon movement in, another security. (Although this book focuses on equity options, those are not the only types of options available.) Often you see the stock in which an option derives its value referred to as the *underlying security*.

When you purchase an equity option contract, you get the right to buy or sell 100 shares of the underlying security. You can take advantage of (or *exercise*) this right, or you can simply sell the option. For example, Google stock is the underlying security for Google options. One option contract typically represents 100 underlying shares. This may change slightly if there is an adjustment or a reorganization of capital in the underlying stock.

Exercise price

The *exercise* (or *strike*) price is the predetermined fixed price at which you can purchase (call) or sell (put) the underlying stock.

Options are available in standardized strike prices at regular intervals. That is, widely traded securities such as Sun Microsystems (SUNW) that are trading at less than $5 per share have a $1 increment strike price. More commonly found strike price increments are as follows:

- $1 increments, for stocks trading at less than $5

- $2.50 increments, for stocks trading at $5 to $25 per share

- $5 increments, for stocks trading at $25 to $200 per share

- $10 increments, for stocks trading at more than $200

Expiration date

An option's *expiration date* designates the last day on which professional traders may exercise that option. Retail traders (you and me) usually have an exercise cut-off of the last trading day before expiration. After an option expires, the option buyer loses the right to buy or sell, and the option contract becomes worthless.

The OCC determines expiration dates. The actual expiration date for stock (equity) options is the Saturday after the third Friday of the expiration month. Trading usually ends at close of business on the third Friday, although this can vary with public holidays and other events.

Option expiration date calendars are available from the OCC Web site (www.theocc.com).

As of October 2006, if an option expires with intrinsic value of $0.05 or more, it may automatically be executed by the Options Clearing Corporation (OCC) — the entity that protects option buyers by making sure options sellers meet their obligations.

If, for example, you own the DIS 25 strike call option, which closed at $25.10 on the last trading day before expiration. At the close, the option would be worth $0.10.

Do nothing, and you still may end up with a surprise in your trading account. The OCC assumes that you didn't want that security to expire worthless and automatically exercises the option for you over the weekend. Hopefully you have the funds to cover the purchase of DIS shares at the $25 exercise price, because that's the transaction that occurs.

Passively managing options is a bad idea in general. Stay on top of them.

Expiration is a relatively straightforward concept but one that requires a thorough understanding. Reach the expiration date, and your contract ceases to exist. In other words, the option holder no longer has any rights, the seller has no obligations, and the contract has no value.

Have you ever heard someone say that 90% of all options expire worthless? That percentage is open to debate — the Chicago Board Options Exchange says the figure is closer to 30%) — but the fact is that options do expire. They have a fixed life, which eventually runs out. To understand why, recall what an options contract is: an agreement between a buyer and a seller. Among other things, the two parties agree on a duration for the contract. The duration of the options contract is based on the expiration date. Once the expiration date has passed, the contract no longer exists. It is worthless.

The concept is similar to a prospective buyer approaching the seller of a house and paying them money to keep the house at the same price for them for the next three months. In that case, the payment gives the individual the right to purchase the home. The seller, however, doesn't want to grant that right forever. For that reason, the payment gives the owner the right to buy the home, but only for a predetermined period of time. After that time has elapsed, the agreement is void; the seller keeps the payment, and can then attempt to sell the house to another prospective buyer.

Option premiums

The *premium* (or price of the option) is the compensation paid by the option buyer to the option seller (or option writer). Option premiums vary as:

- ✔ They near expiration (time value shrinks).
- ✔ The price of the underlying security changes.
- ✔ Change in interest rates — the higher the interest rate, the larger the option premium.
- ✔ Volatility fluctuates.

The potential loss on a purchased (long) option is limited to the premium paid, regardless of the underlying stock's price movement. That's why the purchase of an option enables traders to control the amount of risk assumed.

In contrast, the potential profit on a short (sold) option is limited to premium received, regardless of the underlying stock's performance.

Option styles

Two *styles* of options exist: American and European. The difference lies in when you can exercise the option:

✔ You can exercise *American-style* options anytime up to the trading day prior to expiration. Equity options traded in the options market are American style.

✔ You can exercise *European-style* options only on their expiration day. Again, retail traders need to check the specific cut-off time for them to provide exercise instructions to their broker. Typically most Index options are European-style.

Surveying Option Cycles

In general, all options for a particular class follow one of the three quarterly cycles that usually extend out six to nine months. The three cycles are:

✔ Cycle 1: January/April/July/October

✔ Cycle 2: February/May/August/November

✔ Cycle 3: March/June/September/December

Equity options are available for the current month and next month out. Each stock also has options available roughly nine months out, based upon the quarterly expiration cycle in which they fall. Additionally, longer term options such as Long Term Equity Anticipation Securities (LEAPS) are available for a more limited number of actively traded equities and indexes.

The acronym LEAPS stands for Long-Term Equity Anticipation Securities. While the name seems somewhat arcane, LEAPS are nothing more than long-term options. Some investors incorrectly view these long-term options as a separate asset class. But in fact, the only real difference between LEAPS and conventional equity options is the time left until expiration. That is, while short-term options expire within a maximum of eight months, LEAPS can have terms lasting more than 2½ years. Even though the only real distinction between conventional options and LEAPS is the time left until expiration, there are important differences to consider when you implement trading strategies with LEAPS, and one of the most important is the impact of time decay.

The Meat of the Trade

When you get down to the nitty gritty, trading options means opening and closing a contract. Of course, how and when you do that, and what you contract for, make the difference between profit and loss. This section shows you the basics of opening and closing trades.

Opening and closing

When you first buy (or write) an option contract with your broker, it is called an *opening transaction*. If you then sell (or buy) options to exit the position, it is called a *closing transaction*. The *open* and *close* concepts are used when placing orders with your broker. It may sound a little funky at first, but you get used to it quickly.

For example, an instruction to your broker to "Buy to Open 1 September call option for General Electric (GE) with a strike price of $35" is called an *opening transaction*. The number *1* indicates the number of contracts you wish to purchase. If, after one month, you decide you don't want to remain in this position, you would instruct your broker to "Sell to Close 1 September 35 call option" to exit the position. This *closing transaction* has offset the original order.

After the closing transaction has been transacted, the initial open option contract is cancelled and you have no further rights or obligations arising from these GE call option contracts (on either the buy or sell side).

When placing an option order, always tell your broker whether it is an opening or closing transaction.

Exiting a trade

You have three alternatives for exiting an open transaction. Experience is the best teacher when it comes to choosing the best alternative. Because each one produces an immediate result, understanding how to profitably close out a trade is essential to becoming a successful options trader.

A momentary fluctuation in stock price can mean the difference between opportunity and crisis. To make the most of any option, traders with open positions need to keep track of the price of the underlying security each day. Luckily, computers make this process easier and more efficient than ever before.

Recent statistics from the International Securities Exchange (ISE) reveal that around 60% of options are closed out through offsetting before expiration, around 10% are exercised, and around 30% expire worthless.

Offsetting (Closing)

Offsetting is a closing transaction that cancels an open position. Offsetting an option position is the most popular technique of closing an option trade for option buyers.

To offset, you do the opposite of what you did to open transaction. You have four ways to offset an option transaction:

- ✔ If you bought a call, sell the same call.
- ✔ If you sold a call, buy the same call.
- ✔ If you bought a put, sell the same put.
- ✔ If you sold a put, buy the same put.

The best time to offset an option is when there are gains on the position. You may also use offsetting to avoid incurring further losses.

You can offset an option at any time — whether one second after you entered it or one minute left in the trading day before it expires.

Make sure that you know the expiration dates of your open option positions. Otherwise, you may end up leaving a nice profit on the table.

Exercising

When you *exercise* a long option position, you close your open position by taking ownership (call) or delivering (put) the underlying shares at the option's strike price.

You exercise a long call option only if the stock price is above the option's strike price. When you exercise your long call option (rather than close it), here's what happens:

1. Notify your broker that you want to exercise your option. Your broker then notifies the Options Clearing Corporation (OCC).

2. The OCC randomly selects a broker with customers who have written (sold) call options in that series. On the following day, the broker notifies the writer that her obligation is due and she must deliver to the OCC the corresponding number of shares in the underlying stock.

3. Your trading account is debited the purchase price of a 100 shares (per contract) in the underlying stock at the call strike price.

4. You now own the underlying shares at the call strike price.

This seamless process happens even more quickly now with technology advances. At some point, you may find the transaction occurs on the same day you submit exercise instructions.

You exercise a put option only if the stock price is below the option's strike price. When you exercise your long put option (rather than close it), here's what happens:

1. Notify your broker that you want to exercise your option. Your broker then notifies the Options Clearing Corporation (OCC).

2. The OCC randomly selects a broker with customers who have written (sold) put options in that series. On the following day the broker notifies the writer that her obligation is due and she must buy via the OCC the corresponding number of shares in the underlying stock.

Avoiding selling what you don't really own

The OCC assumes you don't want your security options to expire and can automatically exercise the option for you if you don't do something about it by the expiration date. Sometimes when OCC automatically exercises an option on your behalf, strange things can happen: If you aren't careful, you could end up obliged to sell stock you don't even own!

If you own a call option, and the OCC exercises it on your behalf because you neglect to pay attention to the expiration date, you may end up buying a stock you didn't mean to, which isn't a wonderful surprise. But neglecting a put option could be worse.

A put option that is auto-exercised by the OCC results in the sale of shares. What if you didn't own the stock already? Guess who's now short stock? Now that's an even bigger surprise, and not a good one. You have gone from a limited risk position to one that has unlimited risk. You must be actively involved in managing your account.

If you do not wish the OCC to auto-exercise a long option that may be worth more than $0.05 at expiration you need to contact your broker and provide specific instructions to that effect to avoid having this happen. Check with your broker for instruction cut-off times.

3. Your trading account is credited the value of 100 shares (per contract) in the underlying stock at the put option strike price.

4. Your shares are sold via the OCC at the put strike price.

You can exercise an American option at any time before expiration; but if you exercise an option, you typically don't do it until just prior to expiration.

An option writer cannot exercise an option. By writing an option, you are taking the risk of having a buyer exercise the option against you if the market price movement makes it an in-the-money (ITM) option.

Letting an option expire

You let an option *expire* when the option is out-of-the-money (OTM) or worthless close to the expiration date.

Letting short options expire is the cheapest way to realize a profit. If you let a short option expire, you get to keep the premium you received when you opened the position.

Getting a handle on assignment

Assignment is one of the more confusing processes of an option. Although it occurs infrequently, it's an important part of basic option mechanics. All option traders need to have a solid understanding of assignment in order to maximize their chances for success.

Assignment is the term used to describe the option writer's (seller's) obligation to sell or buy the underlying stock at the strike price at which they sold the option contract. The buyer of an option has the right (but not the obligation) to exercise the option — to buy the underlying stock at the strike price for a long call or to sell the underlying stock at the strike price for a long put.

Typically, most option writers don't want to be assigned at expiration, because most of these strategies rely on taking in an initial premium, then pocketing it when expiration arrives. It's generally not their intention to sell (call) or buy (put) the underlying security, which requires a large cash outlay and puts them in a position that's counter to the direction of market.

If your short position looks like it has any chance of expiring in-the-money, and therefore not expiring worthless, you should close out your short position and avoid the risk of assignment.

How do you know that you're at risk of being assigned? First, remember that exercise generally takes place only with in-the-money options. Consider also the amount of time value left in the option. When an option is exercised before expiration, it's known as early or premature exercise. In general, if there is time value (¼-point or more) left in the option, the option won't be exercised. Option sellers can expect assignment when the option has little-to-no time value remaining.

Running Down Contract Specifications

The options this chapter discusses are known as *standardized* options because the terms and conditions for the option follow certain requirements from the OCC. That means the strike price, expiration terms, and manner in which the security trades comply with specific defined formats. As a result, you can buy and sell these options on different exchanges without having to worry about whether the DIS Sep 25 call option you purchased on the American Stock Exchange can be sold on the Chicago Board Options Exchange. It can; standardized equity options are all cleared and guaranteed through the OCC.

The terms for equity option contracts are also referred to as *specifications* and include information about the option style and expiration periods. One of the advantages of trading these options is that their terms are standard and clearly definable. Table 1-1 outlines the major features of equity options.

Table 1-1	Equity Options Features
Underlying equity	Any stock approved by the OCC with options available.
Security code	The first one to three characters are the equity option code (such as GE) and the last two characters define the options type and expiration month and the strike price.
Multiplier	100. Each option package generally reflects a multiplier of 100.
Exercise style	American-style (that is, exercisable anytime before expiration day.)
Strike prices	1, 2.5- and 5-point intervals.
Type	Call and put options.
Expiration day	The Saturday following the third Friday of the month.

Last trading day	The market close on the trading day immediately before expiration Saturday, usually the third Friday.
Trading hours	9:30 a.m. to 4:00 p.m. Eastern Time.
Settlement	Equity options are settled using the closing price on the last day of trading prior to expiration for the equity.
Settlement day	The first business day following the last trading day.

Going Long, Going Short

A good understanding of the terms *long* and *short* is critical for beginning traders. You may find the concepts a little confusing until you get the hang of them, but the concepts are absolutely essential for every trader.

Going long

Going long describes a position in which you have purchased and own a security. For example, if you have purchased the right to buy 100 shares of a security, you are long one call option contract. If you have purchased the right to sell 100 shares of a security, you are long one put option contract. If you have purchased 100 shares of a security outright you are simply long 100 shares.

Going short

Going short describes a position in which you have sold a security you don't own. In return, you now have the obligations inherent in the terms of the short stock or option contract. For example, if you have sold the right to buy 100 shares of a stock to someone else, you are short one call option contract. If you have sold the right to sell 100 shares of a stock to someone else, you are short one put option contract. When you write an option contract, you are in a sense, creating it. The writer of an option collects and keeps the premium received from its initial sale.

Digging into short and long

Going long and going short are easily confused terms, especially when you're dealing with put options. For example, if you are short put options, you are in effect long or bullish the underlying instrument. Table 1-2 provides a quick reference to the terms and how they relate to options.

Table 1-2	Market opportunity matrix			
	Stock		**Option**	
Market View	*Buy/Sell*	*Long/Short*	*Buy/Sell*	*Long/Short*
Bullish	Buy stock	Long stock	Buy call	Long call
			Sell put	Short put
Bearish	Sell stock	Short stock	Buy put	Long put
			Sell call	Short call

When it comes to taking advantage of various market conditions, options strategies will enable you to expand your creativity immeasurably.

Going long calls and puts provide the basics of options trading, but only when you begin to combine long and short options, or combine options with the underlying asset, can you begin to unlock the tremendous power of options trading.

Chapter 2

Types of Trades and the Risk Within

. . . .

In This Chapter

▶ Uncovering calls and puts

▶ Decoding risk profiles

▶ Call options: Going long, going short

▶ The long and short of put options

. . . .

*E*ach type of option trade comes with its own set of bene-fits and risks. Assessing risk is an important factor in all aspects of trading, and options are no exception. By compar-ing the risk-reward prospects for a trade you can determine the best option strategy for current market condition. This chapter gives you the skinny on the kinds of trades you can make and helps you evaluate the risks associated with each.

Deciphering Call Options

Call options are an attractive alternative to buying stock. Call options give the buyer the right, but not the obligation to buy an underlying stock at the call's strike price. In the United States, each stock option generally represents 100 shares of the underlying stock.

A call option works like this:

> ✔ Purchasing a call option effectively locks in a particular price on the underlying stock and allows the buyer to enjoy the same advantage of unlimited profit potential that comes with owning 100 shares of the underlying stock.

> ✔ A call option holder has the right, if he or she chooses, to purchase a stock, index, or futures contract at the option strike price until the option's expiration.
>
> ✔ The option seller (writer) has the obligation to fulfill that right.

A call option holder has the right to choose, and the call option seller has the obligation to fulfill.

Options are available in various strike prices (see Chapter 1) depending on the current market price of the underlying security. Expiration dates can vary from the current month out to more than 2½ years for some January options.

Here's an example of a call option purchased by a trader:

1 x October BNI 55 Call @ 1.45

This purchase is known as a *long* position. Similar to stock, when a trader buys the security it is referred to as *going long*. It represents the standard transaction order, buying a security first, and later selling it, as opposed to going short, in which you borrow shares and sell them without actually owning them.

This long option breaks down as follows:

> ✔ It gives the purchaser the right to buy 100 shares of BNI at $55 per share ($5,500 total).
>
> ✔ That right is good until the end of the last trading day before expiration Saturday in October.
>
> ✔ The cost to acquire this right is the premium of $145 ($1.45 x 100 shares = $145).

Stock options have various strike intervals depending on the price range of the stock. Although there may be additional strike prices available because of corporate activity (mergers, splits, or dividends), common strike price increments include the following:

Increment	*Security price range*
$1	Usually less than $5
$2.50	$5 to $25
$5	$25 to $200

Just as the price of a stock fluctuates daily, so does the price of an option. The relationship between the strike price of a call and the price of the underlying security determines whether a call is referred to as *in-the-money, out-of-the-money,* or *at-the-money.* The general term *moneyness* is used when discussing this price-strike price relationship. Table 2-1 illustrates how moneyness works. (See Chapter 4 for more details.)

Table 2-1	Call option moneyness
Derivative versus Underlying Price	**Money Position**
Call strike price < Stock price	In-the-money (ITM) option
Call strike price = Stock price	At-the-money (ATM) option
Call strike price >Stock price	Out-of-the-money (OTM) option

Interpreting Put Options

Put options give the buyer the right, but not the obligation, to sell shares of an underlying security at a fixed price until the option's expiration date. Buying a put option is a welcome alternative to short selling a stock. Although both strategies offer traders the chance to make a profit from a declining market, only buying a put does so with limited risk.

When you sell a stock short, you reverse the order of a standard transaction by borrowing shares from your broker and selling them in the market first, then buying back the stock at a later time.

A put option holder has the right, if she chooses, to sell the stock at a set price within a certain time period. The option writer (seller) has the obligation to fulfill that right.

A put option holder has the right to sell, and the put option seller has an obligation to buy.

Just like call options, put options come in various strike prices with a variety of expiration dates. However, unlike call options, if you are *bearish* (expect the stock price to fall), you might consider going long a put option. If you were *bullish* (expect the stock price to rise) you might consider going short a put option.

Here's an example of a long put option:

1 October BNI 50 Put @ 0.60

Here's how the example put option breaks down:

- ✔ It gives the purchaser the right to sell 100 shares of BNI at $50.00 per share ($5,000 total).

- ✔ That right is good until the end of the last trading day before expiration Saturday in October.

- ✔ The cost to acquire this right is the premium of $60 (0.60 x 100 = $60).

As I explain in the section "Deciphering Call Options," strikes for stock options come in multiples of $1, $2.50, and $5, depending on the underlying stock value as defined by the exchange.

The relationship between the strike price of a put and the price of the underlying security determines whether a put is in-the-money, out-of-the-money, or at-the-money (see Chapter 4). Table 2-2 shows how the relationship plays out.

Table 2-2   Put option moneyness

Derivative versus underlying price	Money position
Put strike price >Stock price	In-the-money (ITM) option
Put strike price = Stock price	At-the-money (ATM) option
Put strike price < Stock price	Out-of-the-money (OTM) option

A bearish trader may purchase a put (go long) because he expects the underlying stock to decrease in price. The trader will most likely make a profit if the market price of the underlying security decreases fast enough to overcome the put option's time decay.

Making Sense of Risk Profiles

A *risk profile,* or risk graph, is a visual representation of the profit or loss of a position in relation to price changes in the underlying security. When drawn with software, risk profiles can also take into account the effects of changes in time and volatility (see Chapter 4) of the position. Risk profiles enable traders to visually assess a trade's profitability in one glance.

Successful traders always look at the "what if I am wrong" scenario before looking at any potential profit that they can make on a trade. By creating a risk profile for each potential trade, you can visually assess its profit and loss specifics.

Figure 2-1 shows a risk profile for a long call option that has been computer-generated by Optionetics Platinum, an options trading and analysis software program.

The horizontal numbers at the bottom of the graph show the underlying security's price. The vertical numbers on the left show profit and loss values in dollars. The black sloping graph line indicates the theoretical profit and loss of the position at expiration, as it corresponds to the price of the underlying security. The other three more curved sloping lines take into account the theoretical value of the position at different times prior to expiration.

The call option in Figure 2-1 was purchased with a strike price of 30 at a premium of $2.95, or $295, for one contract. There are 149 days left for the call option. The maximum risk is equal to the call premium paid, in this case $295. The maximum reward is unlimited — just as if you owned the underlying stock.

You don't need a computer program to calculate the basics of a risk profile; they can be drawn by hand by calculating the maximum risk and reward for most option strategies at expiration. However, if you want to go that next step and calculate what an option's position will be worth at any time prior to expiration or what it will be worth given a change in volatility, then you need a software tool to calculate and draw it.

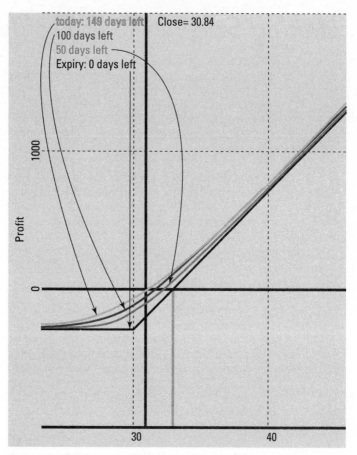

today: 149 days left   Close= 30.84
100 days left
50 days left
Expiry: 0 days left

Profit

1000

0

30   40

Figure 2-1: The risk profile for a long call option

Going Long Calls

If you choose to *go long* (buy) a call option, you purchase the right to buy the underlying instrument at the strike price you choose up until the day before expiration, usually the 3rd Friday of the expiration month. (Turn to Chapter 1 to find out more.)

A long call has the following position characteristics:

- ✔ **Limited risk:** Limited to the premium paid for the call option.

- ✔ **Breakeven:** Call strike price plus the call premium. When the underlying security reaches this price level, the option position has neither gains nor losses at expiration; in other words, the option can be sold just prior to expiration for the same amount it was purchased.

- ✔ **Unlimited profit:** Unlimited to the upside beyond the breakeven. The profit is based on the performance of the underlying security, so the call profit increases as the price of the underlying security rises above the strike price. Because the stock has no real limit to its upside potential, your potential profit is unlimited.

- ✔ **Risk profile:** Shows an unlimited profit above the breakeven and limited loss below the breakeven, as the solid line in Figure 2-2 shows.

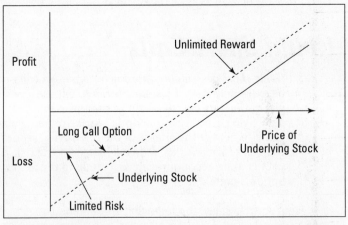

Figure 2-2: A long call has lower associated risk than a stock but similar potential for profit.

You take a long call option position when you expect the underlying stock to go up in value. The premium you pay for the long call option shows up as a debit in your trading account and is the maximum loss you risk by purchasing the call.

In contrast, the maximum profit of a long call option is unlimited depending on how high the underlying instrument rises in price (the upside) above the strike price. As the underlying stock rises, the long call increases in value because it gives the option holder the right to buy the underlying stock at its lower strike price. That's why you want to go long a call option in a rising or bull market.

A bullish trader may purchase a call (go long) because she expects the stock to increase in price. The trader will most likely make a profit if the market price of the underlying security increases fast enough to overcome the call option's time decay.

Options are a *wasting asset:* Their value declines as they approach expiration. Owning the underlying stock has no expiration.

Because calls can be purchased at a fraction of the price of buying the stock, they're an economical way to leverage trading capital in order to participate in market movement.

Going Short Calls

Going short (also called *shorting* or *writing*) a call option can be extremely risky. By selling a call to initiate a position, you grant someone else the right to purchase 100 shares of the underlying security at the option strike price. You are obligated to deliver the shares of the underlying security *even if you don't currently own it.* In exchange for the risk you assume, your trading account receives a credit in the amount of the option's premium.

A short call has the following characteristics:

> ✔ **Unlimited risk:** After the stock moves above the breakeven price, the risk begins to increase. Because a stock can continue to move higher indefinitely, the risk is technically unlimited.

✔ **Breakeven:** Call strike price plus the call premium. When the underlying security reaches this price level, the option position has neither gains nor losses at expiration.

✔ **Limited profit:** Limited to the premium received for selling the call option. Selling a call enables traders to profit from a decrease in the underlying market. If the underlying stock stays below the strike price until the option's expiration, the option expires worthless and the trader gets to keep the credit received.

✔ **Risk profile:** Shows a limited profit above the breakeven and unlimited loss below the breakeven, as the solid line in Figure 2-3 shows.

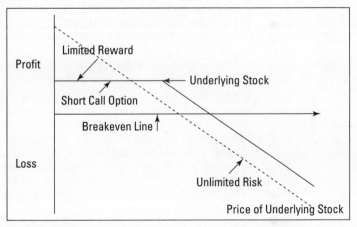

Figure 2-3: Going short presents unlimited risk but limited profit.

The maximum loss of a short call is unlimited and depends on how high the price of the underlying security rises to the upside beyond the call's strike price. If the underlying stock rises above a short call's strike price, the call buyer is likely to exercise the option. In that case

✔ The call writer is obligated to deliver 100 shares of the underlying security at the call's strike price to the call buyer.

✔ The option seller keeps the premium she received when she originally wrote the call, and she can use it to offset part or all of her loss from having to buy the underlying stock at a higher price to fulfill this obligation.

If the price of the underlying stock remains lower than the call strike price, the call is not in danger of being assigned. An option buyer has no reason to exercise a call option when he can buy the underlying stock at a lower current market price.

However, if the price of the underlying stock rises above the strike price, the owner will likely exercise the call, and it is assigned to the call seller. The call seller is then obligated to sell 100 shares of the underlying stock per call contract at this lower value (the option strike price).

A short call position can be quite expensive, which is why experts never recommend selling *naked* or *uncovered* options (those that you don't own sufficient shares of the underlying security to cover). Experienced traders who choose to short call options often do so as part of a hedged combination options strategy.

Selling naked calls is restricted by brokerages. The highest level of option approval is required along with high margin deposits — which demonstrates just how risky naked options can be if you use them in isolation. However, a short call can be very useful in hedging and combination options strategies, and therefore you need to understand its basic properties.

Although options are listed in the financial pages of most major newspapers, the list is not complete due to limited space available in a paper. It is much easier to find options quotes at various sites on the Internet such as your broker, Optionetics, or the exchanges.

Going Long Puts

If you choose to buy or *go long* a put option, you are purchasing the right to sell the underlying security at a specific strike price on or before the specified expiration date of the option. The premium of the long put option shows up as a debit in your trading account.

Going long a put option has the following characteristics:

- ✔ **Limited risk:** Limited to the premium paid for the put option.

- ✔ **Breakeven:** Put strike price minus the put premium. When the underlying security reaches this price level, the option position has neither gains nor losses at expiration.

- ✔ **Limited profit:** Limited potential to the downside beyond the breakeven. The put profit increases as the price of the underlying security falls below the strike price, but has a limited range because the underlying stock can only fall to zero.

- ✔ **Risk profile:** Shows a limited profit above the breakeven and a limited loss below the breakeven equal to the premium paid to purchase the option.

You take a long put position when the underlying stock is expected to go down in value. As the underlying stock falls, the long put becomes more valuable because it gives you the right to sell the underlying stock at the higher strike price. That's why you want to go long put options in a bearish or falling market.

The risk profile in Figure 2-4 shows how a long put option's risk is limited to the cost of the premium, whereas a short stock comes with unlimited risk as the stock climbs above its initial price. Both trading instruments enjoy limited profit potential as the underlying stock falls toward zero.

Because you can typically purchase puts for less than you would pay to short the underlying stock, puts are an economical way to leverage trading capital in order to participate in market movement.

Long put positions can also be used to insure a stock position against a downturn in the markets. For example, when Enron stock plummeted due to corporate scandal, had you correctly owned Enron stock with puts, your loss may have been as little as $.50 per share!

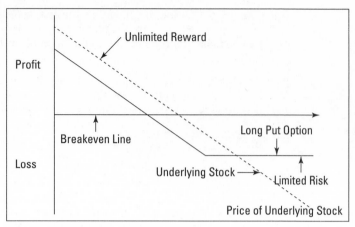

Figure 2-4: The value of a long put rises as the price of the underlying stock falls.

Going Short Puts

Going short (or *writing*) a put option is risky. When you sell a put option you give someone else the right (but not the obligation) to sell 100 shares of the underlying security at the option's strike price until the expiration date.

You're the one who is obligated to comply with the terms of the contract. In the case of a put, you're obligated to purchase the stock — it's put to you. In exchange for assuming this risk, you receive a credit in the amount of the option's premium.

A short put has the following characteristics:

- ✔ **Limited, but high-risk:** Limited risk because the price of the underlying stock can only fall to zero.

- ✔ **Breakeven:** Put strike price minus the put premium. When the underlying security reaches this price level, the option position has neither gains nor losses at expiration.

- **Limited profit:** Limited to the premium received for selling the put option. By selling a put option, you receive the option's premium in the form of a credit into your trading account. The premium received is the maximum reward for a short put position. In most cases, you anticipate that the short put will expire worthless.

- **Risk profile:** Shows a profit limited to the put premium received and a limited loss below the breakeven (as the underlying stock can only fall to zero).

  If the price of the underlying stock remains higher than the strike price of the put, you aren't in danger of the put being exercised. An option buyer has no reason to exercise a put option when he can sell the underlying stock at a higher current market price.

However, if the price of the underlying stock falls below the strike price, the put seller may exercise the put. The put seller is then obligated to purchase 100 shares per put contract at the higher strike price.

If your put option is exercised, you are obligated to purchase the underlying security at the strike price sold. Experienced traders who choose to go short put options do so in a stable or bull market because the put will not be exercised unless the market falls. There is also a substantial margin requirement for shorting puts.

The risk profile in Figure 2-5 shows the difference between a short put providing limited reward and the long stock offering unlimited reward. Both trading instruments come with limited, but high risk, which is why experts never recommend trading a naked put (see the section "Going Short Calls," earlier in this chapter, for more detail).

The risk for a short put is technically limited, but it is so high that sometimes traders consider it "unlimited," especially when you consider the risk-reward relationship. A very high risk, paired with a very low and limited reward adds up to, well, a risk so high you might as well call it unlimited.

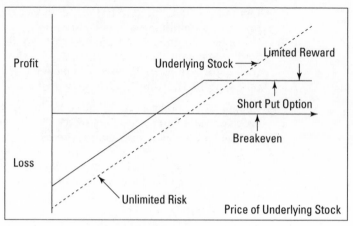

Figure 2-5: The risk for a short put is limited, but high as the stock declines.

Chapter 3

Understanding Option Quotes

*O*ption symbols and quotes are a kind of shorthand that provides important details about a particular option. This information is readily recognized by experienced traders, but somewhat indecipherable to beginners. This chapter shows you how to read option symbols and quotes to de-code the vast data being provided.

The Internet has made the process of reviewing option prices extremely easy. Dozens of sites provide quote services, and some of these services provide real-time quotes (but most are delayed by at least 20 minutes). The exchange Web sites are good resources for free, delayed stock and option quotes. If you want to receive streaming real-time data, you must be willing to pay for it. Some brokers include this as part of their service, so it pays to ask.

Check out the following Web sites for five of the major option exchanges:

▸ The American Stock Exchange (www.amex.com)

▸ The Boston Options Exchange (www.bostonoptions.com)

▸ The Chicago Board Options Exchange (www.cboe.com)

✔ The International Securities Exchange (www.iseoptions.com)

✔ The Philadelphia Stock Exchange (www.phlx.com)

Figuring Out Option Symbols

Option symbols are generally three- to five-character-length codes issued by the exchange or Option Clearing Corporation (OCC). When you consider all of the stocks with listed options, the two types of options available, and all of the strike prices possible, there are a ton of option symbols in existence on any given day. As a result, they are generally re-used after they expire.

The first portion of the symbol is known as the option root and it identifies the underlying stock. When possible, the option root is the same as the stock symbol. Since the option root is limited to three characters and over-the-counter (OTC) stocks are identified by a four-character symbol, the option root for these stocks must be different.

After the option root, the option type (call or put), expiration month, and strike price are provided. The second-to-last character designates both the option type and expiration month, while the last character designates the strike price. This becomes easier to understand when you review the example that follows.

When speaking with a broker you often find that even if you refer only to the option symbol, the broker nevertheless typically uses more-descriptive language to define the option. Your broker wants to be sure that you're both discussing the same security and to avoid any mistakes that might be made by repeating the wrong option code.

When you discuss options, do like the brokers: Be specific. Use the following option details:

✔ Underlying stock

✔ Expiration month

✔ Strike price

✔ Type (call or put)

For example, "GE September 35 call" has the code GEIG and is broken down as follows:

Option Code	Underlying Stock	Expiration Month	Strike Price	Type
GEIG	GE	September	35	Call

The second to last symbol ("I" in the example) designates both the expiration month and the type of option (call or put). Table 3-1 provides you with the call and put symbols for each month.

Table 3-1   Option Expiration Month Codes

Month	Call	Put
Jan	A	M
Feb	B	N
Mar	C	O
Apr	D	P
May	E	Q
Jun	F	R
Jul	G	S
Aug	H	T
Sep	I	U
Oct	J	V
Nov	K	W
Dec	L	X

The last symbol ("G" in the example) designates the strike price for the option. Because the range of potential strike prices is pretty large, the table in Figure 3-1 provides a partial list of strike symbols to give you a feel for how it works.

A	B	C	D	E	F	G	H	I	J	K	L	M
5	10	15	20	25	30	35	40	45	50	55	60	65
105	110	115	120	125	130	135	140	145	150	155	160	165
N	O	P	Q	R	S	T	U	V	W	X	Y	Z
70	75	80	85	90	95	100	7.5	12.5	17.5	22.5	27.5	32.5
170	175	180	185	190	195	200	–	–	–	–	–	–

Figure 3-1: Select Option Strike Price Codes

What you see isn't always what you get with option quotes. Prior to placing the trade, always verify any quote you are interested in trading with your broker. If something looks wrong with the premium, have the broker check for a current quote as well as the specifications for the symbol.

Decoding Option Quotes

When you look up an option quote, you get quite a bit of information. Here's a rundown of the terms that you typically encounter:

- ✓ **Symbol/Code:** The unique identifier assigned to the option by the OCC for trading, clearing and settlement purposes.

- ✓ **Expiration:** The last date an option may be exercised by any market participant. All unexercised options cease to exist on this day. The exercise cut-off for most retail traders (you and me) is usually the last trading day before expiration.

- ✓ **Bid:** The highest price a prospective buyer is prepared to pay for a trading unit of a specified security. If there is a high demand for the underlying security, the prices are bid up to a higher level. Retail traders generally sell at the bid price.

- ✓ **Ask:** The lowest price acceptable to a prospective seller of a security. A low demand for a stock translates to the market being offered down to the lowest price at which a person is willing to sell. Retail traders generally buy at the ask price.

- ✔ **Bid-ask spread:** Together, the bid and ask prices constitute the quote, and the difference between the two prices is the bid-ask spread. The bid-ask dynamic is common to all stocks and options.

- ✔ **Last:** The last price at which the option traded. For delayed quotes, this price may not reflect the actual price of the option at the time you view the quote.

- ✔ **Volume:** The total number of contracts traded that day.

- ✔ **Open interest:** The total number of outstanding contracts currently in the market. The value reflects the prior day's tally. It also defines an option's liquidity; the higher the number, the easier it is to move in and out of a trade.

Exploring a Sample Quote

Option quotes are similar to stock quotes and vary by source. Free quotes may be delayed by 15 to 20 minutes, so be sure you determine whether you are viewing delayed or real-time information. Table 3-2 displays a detailed option quote for company XYZ that gives you a snapshot of how that option is performing.

Table 3-2	Sample Option Quote for XYZ Company		
XYZ AH		*XYZ Jan 40 Call*	
Day's Range:	$1.05 - $1.35	Prev. Close:	$1.10
Bid:	$1.30	Volume:	529
Ask:	$1.35	Open Interest:	3,004
Last:	$1.20	Expiration:	1/21/07

Generally the detailed quote includes the option symbol along with its description. Price information includes the trading range for the day, the current bid and ask, as well as the price of the last trade. Many detailed quote screens will also provide you with the closing price from the previous trading day and some may also provide the change in value (not displayed here).

In addition to price data, information regarding the trading volume for the day, the total number of contracts for the option (Open Interest) and the specific expiration date are also provided.

Chapter 4

How Options Earn Their Worth

*B*efore you delve into options trading, you need to understand how the market determines the value of an option. A whole slew of factors come into play; these are plugged into a mathematical formula to arrive at a theoretical price. Market forces of supply and demand also impact the price you ultimately see in a quote. This chapter gives you an overview of what makes an option worth whatever it's worth.

Digging Into Option Value

Eight major components affect an option's value. The following sections describe them and explain a little about how they play into an option's price.

Call or put

Although calls and puts provide different rights to the contract owner, the factors that impact pricing for both are the same. And yet, a call and a put with the same strike price, the same underlying security, and the same expiration have different prices. How can this be? The two primary influences in option pricing are

- ✔ The relationship between the strike price and the price of the underlying.
- ✔ The type of option contract — call or put — being priced.

Underlying stock price and strike price

The major factor that determines the price of any option is its *moneyness*. That is, the price of the underlying stock relative to the *strike* (exercise) price of the option.

The relationship between these two values determines the intrinsic value (see the section "Gauging intrinsic (real) value" later in this chapter) of the option, as well as how far *in-the-money* or *out-of-the-money* a given option is located (see the section "Determining Intrinsic and Extrinsic Value," later in this chapter, for definitions of these terms).

A move in the price of the stock will have a different effect on the option depending on the type of option and the chosen strike price.

Volatility of the underlying stock

Volatility is a percentage that measures the amount by which the underlying stock is expected to change in a given period of time.

Highly volatile stocks have a better chance of making a substantial move than those that aren't so volatile. They offer larger up and down swings in price in shorter time spans than less-volatile stocks. Large movements are attractive to option traders who are always looking for big directional swings to make their contracts profitable. Options of volatile stocks therefore generally command higher premiums than those that are less volatile.

Check out Chapter 5 to find out more about volatility.

Dividends on the underlying stock

Although each variable is important, dividends are often over-looked. Dividends can play an important role in the pricing of options especially around *ex-dividend time*.

Ex-dividend refers to the point when a stock no longer provides rights to a new shareholder of record for a scheduled dividend payment. After the specified ex-dividend date, option prices reflect the reduced value of the stock, as appropriate.

If the dividend is paid out before an option expires, the value of that option accounts for this reduction sooner than later. The impact you see on option prices usually occurs at the ex-dividend time rather than the dividend payment time.

Expiration date

The amount of time remaining until expiration is an extremely important factor for determining option price. The longer an option has until expiration, the greater the chance it has of becoming profitable, and hence the higher the option premium.

American-style or European-style

An *American-style* option permits the exercise of the option at any time prior to expiration, whereas a *European-style* option permits exercise only on the day the option expires. Both types of contracts can be traded at any time.

American-style options carry a slightly higher premium because the exercise feature adds flexibility. In the real trading world, however, you don't typically have a choice as to which type of option to purchase. Typically, equity options are American-style and index options are European-style.

Risk-free rate of return

The risk-free rate of return (usually the US Treasury Bill interest rate) is a factor, but for near-term options (six months or less) it is a marginal one. The actions of the interest rate markets typically have little effect on the price of an individual option.

Higher interest rates can increase call option premiums, whereas lower interest rates can lead to a decrease in call option premiums. The reverse is true for puts — higher interest rates can decrease put option premiums, whereas lower rates increase them.

The risk-free rate is one factor in an option pricing formula and represents the discount rate for the expected future value of the option. Thus, if there isn't much time left until expiration, a change in the risk-free rate doesn't affect the option price significantly.

Demystifying Option Pricing Models

An *option pricing model* is a mathematical process used to determine the theoretical fair-value of an option. By inserting the components in the section "Digging Into Option Value" into a pricing model, a trader can determine what an option should be theoretically worth.

Black-Scholes versus the Binomial: Two competing pricing models

A pricing model is different from a basic calculation because it involves a series of assumptions and calculations. There are two models most often used for pricing equity options. Because you have access to both of these models, it's important to have a basic understanding of how they differ.

✔ **The Black Scholes Model:** First proposed by Black and Scholes in 1973, this Nobel winning prize paper addresses pricing for European-style options. It serves as the foundation for many derivative pricing models.

The main drawback of the Black-Scholes Model is that it does not address early exercise conditions of American-style options. Since this represents most of the equity options today, it's important to note.

✔ **The Binomial Model:** First proposed by Cox, Ross, and Rubinstein in a 1979 paper, this model overcame the early exercise issues with the Black-Scholes Model and American-style options. Today, it's the most commonly used model for valuing equity options.

The price at which an option trades may bear no resemblance to its theoretical model price because the market forces of supply and demand are ultimately the deciding factor.

Various trader assumptions determine a model price — factors like volatility levels, dividend payments, and future interest rates. Different expectations for these components may dramatically alter the model price. As a result, many views about the proper theoretical value of a particular option might exist at any given time.

Although the model price of an option may be close to the current market price, the model price is basically an estimate of an option's value.

In practice, supply and demand often dictate an option's price in the market. Nonetheless, calculating the model price of an option is valuable because it gives you an indication of whether the current market price is higher or lower than the theoretical value, which may also be referred to as the fair value.

The Chicago Board Options Exchange provides a pricing calculator on its Web site (www.cboe.com) that uses a proprietary model to determine option values. You can input the pricing factor values discussed in this chapter to determine a theoretical option price or you can use the current market value of the option to determine the volatility level implied by the market.

In the following minitable, you can see the inputs applied to the CBOE option pricing calculator for Alcoa (AA) options. When you enter the underlying stock symbol in the model, the calculator automatically provides pricing inputs including the option style, price of the underlying stock, current interest rate, and dividend data, as shown here:

Style:	American
Price:	28.36
Strike:	30
Days to expiration:	26
Volatility %:	23.03*
Interest rate %:	3.6094

Dividends date:	August 3, 2007
Dividends amount:	0.56
Dividends frequency:	Quarterly

Note: Volatility can be an input value or can be calculated by the model using the market value of the option.

In addition to the inputs that apply to all AA options, the calculator also provides you with specific call and put data for near month options with strike prices closest to the current price of AA. You can change any of these inputs to evaluate different strike prices or expiration months, or to see how a change in interest rates or volatility affects the price of an option.

Based on the inputs provided, the theoretical value of the AA Sep 30 call and AA Sep 30 put are provided in the first portion of Table 4-1. If instead you place the actual market value of the call option in the option calculator (0.15), the Volatility % figure is updated to reflect the implied volatility.

Table 4-1 CBOE Option Pricing Model Results for AA

	Call	Put
Symbol	AAIF	AAUF
Value	0.1891	1.7707
Implied Volatility		
	Option Price	New Volatility %
Call	0.15	21.12

Determining Intrinsic and Extrinsic Value

Intrinsic and extrinsic values are critical building blocks in option pricing; you find them in most options discussions because they are two of the primary determinants of an option's price.

Defining ITM, OTM, and ATM

An option's intrinsic and extrinsic values depend on the current market price of the underlying security relative to the type and strike price of the option. This relationship is called the option's *moneyness*. The three possible relationships to consider are

- **In-the-money (ITM):** A call option is ITM if its strike price is less than the market price of the underlying security. A put option is in-the-money if the strike price is greater than the market price of the underlying security.

- **Out-of-the-money (OTM):** A call option is OTM if its strike price is above the current market price of the underlying security. A put option is out-of-the-money if its strike price is below the current market price of the underlying security.

- **At-the-money (ATM):** A call or put option is ATM when the strike price of the option is roughly the same as the current price of the underlying security.

Gauging intrinsic (real) value

Intrinsic (real) value is the measurement by which the strike price of an option is in-the-money in relation to the current price of the underlying stock. Here's how you find an option's intrinsic value:

- **For a call option:** Subtract the strike price from the price of the underlying security.

- **For a put option:** Subtract the price of the underlying security from the strike price.

Intrinsic value can never be negative. No matter how much time is left before the option expires, the intrinsic value for an in-the-money option is the difference between the strike price and the price of the underlying security, which is why intrinsic value is also referred to as *real value.*

Figure 4-1 shows you intrinsic value for a call option.

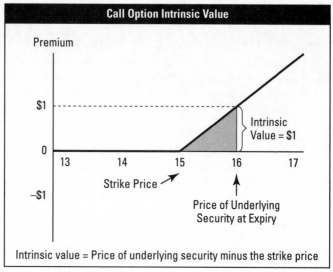

Figure 4-1: The shaded area represents the intrinsic value of a call option.

Figure 4-2 shows you intrinsic value for a put option.

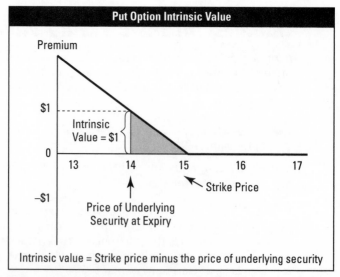

Figure 4-2: The shaded area represents the intrinsic value of a put option.

Determining extrinsic (time) value

Extrinsic (time) value is the amount by which the price of an option exceeds its intrinsic value. Extrinsic value, which is more commonly known as time value, decays over time. In other words, the time value of an option is directly related to how much time the option has until expiration. Four main factors influence the time value of an option (all of which are covered in more depth in the rest of this book):

- ✔ Time to expiration
- ✔ Interest rate
- ✔ Volatility
- ✔ Liquidity

Time value has a snowball effect: The closer an option gets to expiration, the faster the rate of decay in its time value. At a certain point in the life of an option (usually within the last 30 days), its time value starts to decay exponentially. If the market moves in a direction that places the option in-the-money, the option may gain value; however, the time value portion still decreases with the passage of time.

During the life of the option its price is determined by the intrinsic value and the extrinsic value. On expiration day, there is no time (extrinsic) value left to an option. It is worth its intrinsic value only; it's either in-the-money, or it's not. Here's how you determine an option's premium:

Option premiums = Intrinsic Value + Extrinsic value

If a put costs $1.20 and its intrinsic value is $1.00, its time value (extrinsic value) would be $0.20.

($1.20 − $1.00 = $0.20 time value.)

Finding intrinsic and extrinsic value

The time value of an option erodes as the time to expiration gets closer, but the intrinsic value does not erode (providing the stock price remains the same). For a call option, the stock price must be higher than the strike price for the option to have any intrinsic value.

Table 4-2 provides you with a summary of the values impacting a call option price based on moneyness.

Table 4-2	Call Option Moneyness	
Option Position	**Price**	**Value**
ITM	Option strike price < Stock price	Intrinsic value + time value
ATM	Option strike price = Stock price	Time value only
OTM	Option strike price >Stock price	Time value only

For puts, the relationship is just the opposite: The stock price must be lower than the strike price for the option to have any intrinsic value.

Table 4-3 provides you with a summary of the values impacting a put option price based on moneyness.

Table 4-3	Put Option Moneyness	
Position	**Price**	**Value**
ITM option	Option strike price >Stock price	Intrinsic value + Time value
ATM option	Option strike price = Stock price	Time value only
OTM option	Option strike price < Stock price	Time value only

Here's how you calculate the intrinsic value and extrinsic value of a call option. As an example, suppose a company XYZ has the following values for its options:

XYZ shares	$15.50
Call option price	$1.20
Strike price	$15.00
Expiration	In 45 days

You find the intrinsic value by subtracting the strike price from the share price:

$$15.50 - 15.00 = \$0.50$$

You find the extrinsic value by subtracting the intrinsic value from the option price:

$$1.20 - 0.50 = \$0.70$$

In this example, the $15 strike option is ITM with an intrinsic value of $0.50. The extrinsic value as derived from the example is $0.70. As the expiration day approaches (just 45 days away), the time value evaporates.

Out-of-the-money options get cheaper as they move farther OTM. That's because an OTM option consists of nothing but time value; the more out-of-the-money an option is, the less likely it is to move in-the-money by expiration. If the option remains OTM by expiration the option expires worthless. Many inexperienced traders see OTM options as a great deal because of their inexpensive prices. However, the probability that an extremely OTM option will turn profitable is really quite slim.

The deeper in-the-money a call or put option becomes, the less time value and more intrinsic value it has. Because ITM options have less time value, and more intrinsic value, the options premium tends to move along with the price of the underlying security. This relationship is referred to as the *delta of an option* and is the basis for some the most innovative options strategies we offer. Check out Chapter 6 to find out more about delta.

Part II
Options Trading Strategies

"SELL"

In this part . . .

This part goes beyond the basics to reveal more about what you might call the psychology of options trading: I don't mean you can read the mind of the stock market, but you can cope with its mood swings much better when you understand a few simple options strategies. How do you know when an option is about to go up or down in value and how to take advantage of whichever way it's going? How volatile is that option you're holding? Is it more likely to take off or take a dive? Optionetics can help you get a grip on concepts such as *volatility, liquidity*, and *delta change*, and this part shows you how.

This part also covers the most significant piece of the options puzzle: how to place an actual options order the right way with minimal stress! Kick back and relax while reading these sophisticated but easy-to-follow trading pointers because the number one strategy for Optionetics success is trading with confident peace of mind that you're within your risk comfort zone.

Chapter 5

Conditions to Consider: Volatility and Liquidity

*T*wo market conditions, volatility and liquidity, affect your trading decisions. Volatility is one of the most important variables in options trading. It significantly impacts an option's premium and contributes heavily to an option's extrinsic value (see Chapter 4). Liquidity describes the size of a market and gives you a sense of how quickly you can expect to get into and out of a trade. In this chapter, you get the lowdown on both concepts.

Getting the Volatility Picture

Volatility is a measurement of how much an underlying instrument is expected to fluctuate in a given period of time. In other words, it's the speed of change in the market.

Volatility is a crucial element in deciding which strategy to use, and every options trader needs to be well versed on the types of trades that work best for particular volatility levels. A successful options trader always knows which strategy or types of strategies are most appropriate for a particular volatility environment, like a golfer knowing which club to use or a fisherman choosing the best lure.

When the market is volatile, option premiums are inflated and as soon as volatility drops, the price of the option drops, too. You could be right about market direction and still lose because your option premium goes nowhere — or worse, loses value.

Determining volatility before placing a trade increases your chances of making a profit. Knowing volatility can also help determine which strategy is most likely to make money in a specific market — and which strategies to avoid.

As a general rule, traders look at buying strategies during periods of low volatility and look for selling strategies during periods of high volatility. Most novices take the opposite approach, which explains why many beginners lose money trading options.

You need to consider two kinds of volatility — statistical and implied — which I discuss in the following sections.

Introducing statistical volatility

Statistical volatility (also known as historical volatility) represents the standard deviation of a stock's price changes from close-to-close of trading going back a specified number of days.

To determine whether a market is volatile or not, you need to compare current statistical volatility to past levels of statistical volatility.

Volatile markets are ones that exhibit current levels of statistical volatility greater than past levels. Non-volatile markets typically are those in which the current statistical volatility is less than past statistical volatility.

Understanding implied volatility

Implied volatility (IV) is a measure of an underlying stock's volatility, as it's anticipated by the market and reflected in the option's price. In other words, this volatility is *implied* by the option's actual market price and is based partially on the statistical volatility of the underlying stock.

You calculate implied volatility by using the same pricing model you use to calculate the theoretical value of an option. The only difference is you use the current market price of the option as an input to determine the volatility value implied by this price.

Starting with an example using the Alcoa (AA) 30 strike call option for September 2007, here's what you can determine so far about it:

Symbol	AAIF
Style	American
Price	28.36
Strike	30
Expiration date	September 22, 2007
Days to expiration	26
Volatility	23.03%
Interest rate	3.6094%
Dividends date	August 3, 2007
Dividends amount	0.56

Table 5-1 shows the theoretical price of 18.9 cents based on the inputs provided. Notice the volatility value used to calculate this theoretical price is 23.03 percent, which is the current statistical volatility of AAIF. If the AAIF option were sold for at the market price of 15 cents, the implied volatility (IV) of this option would be 21.12 percent. So the volatility implied by the market is slightly less than the historical volatility of the underlying stock.

Table 5-1   Theoretical versus actual option values

	Call	*Put*
Symbol	AAIF	AAUF
Theoretical option value	0.1891	1.7707
Option market value	0.15	1.75

The best thing about implied volatility is that it's very *cyclical;* that is, it tends to move back and forth within a given range. It may remain high or low for a while, and it may reach a new high or low, and then revert to its average.

The key to leveraging implied volatility is knowing that when it actually changes direction, it often moves quickly in the new direction. Buying options when the IV is high and subsequently drops can cause some trades to actually end up losing money even when the price of the underlying security moves in your direction. In this case, you can take advantage of this situation by selling option premium, instead of buying options.

Tracking volatility

Charting both statistical and implied volatility helps option traders to visualize where volatility is relative to the past and relative to each other. Volatility figures don't mean much unless you can compare those figures with the past. This kind of analysis gives the trader some very important information about the market and, specifically, the most appropriate option strategies to employ.

Try to sell options during periods of high volatility and buy options during periods of low volatility.

Figure 5-1 shows a volatility chart of Dell Computers (DELL) representing the statistical (historical) and implied volatility of DELL. You can see that the statistical volatility (black line) of DELL shows a mid-range level of 21.5%, and the average implied volatility (grey line) of DELL options is sitting at the high range of 23.5%.

Buying options when implied volatility is high carries additional risk: If volatility drops, some trades actually end up losing money (even when the price of the underlying security moves in your direction) because that component of the option price declines.

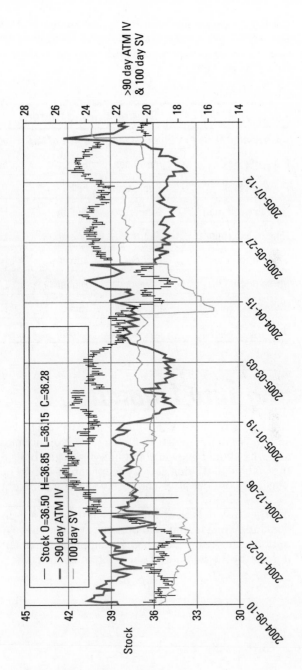

Figure 5-1: DELL volatility and price chart.

Table 5-2 gives you a comprehensive summary of how different factors impact the price of options. Note that sometimes the impact to a call versus a put is the same, while other times it's different.

Table 5-2	Option pricing factors		
Contributing Factor	*Movement*	*Price of Call*	*Price of Put*
Price of stock	Increases	Rise	Fall
Price of stock	Decreases	Fall	Rise
Time to expiration	Longer	Higher	Higher
Time to expiration	Shorter	Lower	Lower
Strike price	Higher	Lower	Higher
Strike price	Lower	Higher	Lower
Underlying volatility	Increases	Higher	Higher
Underlying volatility	Decreases	Lower	Lower

Looking Into Liquidity

Liquidity is the ease with which a security can be bought or sold in the marketplace. But what does liquidity mean to you, and why should you care? Liquidity basically boils down to the volume of trading activity that enables you to buy or sell a security or derivative and receive a fair value for it.

Another way to look at liquidity is in terms of supply and demand. When it comes to options, at-the-money (ATM) options usually have the highest supply and demand (*open interest,* or the number of open option contracts in the market at any one time) because they are less expensive than in-the-money (ITM) options and have a better chance of becoming profitable by expiration than out-of-the-money (OTM) options. (Chapter 4 explains these three conditions of options in depth.)

Options volume, or the total number of contracts traded that day, also affects liquidity. A large number of open contracts together with high trading volume provide good liquidity and a healthy market.

Liquidity gives traders the opportunity to move in and out of a market with ease. ATM options have excellent liquidity because they have a better chance of being profitable than OTM options.

Most of the strategies that you find in this book need to be applied in specific market conditions to be money makers. Liquidity is one of these market conditions. Liquidity is the ease with which a market can be traded. A plentiful number of buyers and sellers increase the volume of trading, producing a liquid market.

If one pit has just a few people hanging out and basically not doing much, and the next pit has hundreds of people fighting for an order, spotting which market has the most liquidity is easy. (It's the busy one.) The bottom line is that plenty of players equates to opportunity.

Reviewing the open interest and volume of a market is an important step of traders and investors. Liquidity enables traders to get their orders filled easily as well as to quickly exit a position. Figure 5-2 provides a snapshot of an XYZ options chain that shows the liquidity (open interest and volume) for some of the available September and October call and put options.

Company XYZ											August 23, 2006	
Mini-quote (delayed)	Last: 33.97						Chg: 0.10		% chg: 0.52%			
Calls							Puts					
Symbol	Open Interest	Volume	Last	Bid	Ask	Strike Price	Bid	Ask	Last	Open Interest	Volume	Symbol
GEIF	4,864	0	4.00	4.00	4.20	30	0	0.05	0	0	31,529	GEUF
GEIZ	6,862	80	1.70	1.60	1.70	32.50	0.05	0.10	0	120	38,566	GEUZ
GEIG	44,952	1,100	0.10	0.10	0.15	35	1.00	1.15	0.05	299	49,728	GEUG
GEIS	57,646	36	0.05	0	0.05	37.50	3.40	3.60	0.75	0	4,798	GEUS
GEJF	0	0	4.00	4.00	4.20	30	0	0.15	3.10	0	0	GEVF
GEJZ	10	95	1.80	1.75	1.90	32.50	0.25	0.35	5.60	75	905	GEVZ
GEJG	1,640	718	0.30	0.35	0.35	35	1.30	1.45	8.10	196	240	GEVG
GEJS	0	0	0	0	0.10	37.50	3.50	3.70	3.60	0	0	GEVS

Figure 5-2: Call option quote with volume and open interest highlighted.

Chapter 6

Demystifying Risk with the Options Greeks

*O*ption traders have a variety of ways to make money trading options. They can profit (or lose) when a stock price moves substantially in one direction or trades in a range; they can also make or lose money when implied volatility increases or decreases. To assess the advantage that one position might have over another, you have to consider the risks involved in each. When making this kind of assessment, options traders typically refer to *delta, gamma, theta,* and *vega*. These four elements of options risk are referred to as *Greeks*.

Introducing the Greeks

The *options Greeks* (named for Greek letters plus Vega, the star) are a set of measurements that quantify an option position's exposure to risk. Options and other trading instruments have a variety of risk exposures that can vary dramatically over time or as markets move. Each of the options Greeks represents a different variable of option pricing.

What about rho?

Rho measures the change in an option's price due to changes in interest rates. Although changes in interest rates occur, over time these changes are very small. The actual impact to price is minimal. You may become interested in rho as you progress as a trader, but for now, you want to focus on the primary Greek elements.

Options and other trading instruments have a variety of risk exposures that can vary dramatically over time or as markets move. Often, it is not enough to know the total risk associated with an option's position. Changes in the price of the underlying instrument trigger changes in the delta, which triggers changes in the rest of the Greeks.

In the beginning, you need to be aware of all of the Greeks, although understanding the delta is the most crucial to your success. Comprehending the definition of each of the Greeks gives you the tools to decipher option pricing. Each of the concepts has a specific use in day-to-day options trading.

- ✔ **Delta:** The change in the price of an option relative to the change of the underlying security. Delta helps you to understand how an option's premium will rise or fall in comparison to the price of the underlying security.

- ✔ **Gamma:** Change in the delta of an option with respect to the change in price of its underlying security. Gamma helps you to gauge the change in an option's delta when the underlying security moves.

- ✔ **Theta:** Change in the price of an option with respect to a change in its time until expiration. Theta measures the amount an option will lose with the passage of one day.

- ✔ **Vega:** Change in the price of an option with respect to its change in volatility. Vega measures the amount an option will gain or lose with a one-percentage point change in the implied volatility of the option.

As the following sections of this chapter explain, all of these terms refer to simple concepts that help you thoroughly understand the risks and potential rewards of option positions. A comprehensive understanding of these concepts can help reduce your risk exposure and stress levels and increase your overall profitability as a trader. Discovering how to integrate these basic concepts into your own trading programs can have a powerful effect on your success as an options trader.

Meeting Delta and Company

Although we could write an entire manual on the option Greeks, in this section we simply introduce the basic concepts.

Delta

Delta refers to the change in the price of an option relative to the change of the underlying security. Another way to think about it is that the delta is the amount by which the price of an option changes for every dollar move in the underlying security. This is a very important number to consider when you construct combination positions.

Call option deltas are positive (0 to 1), and put options have negative deltas (0 to –1). If a call option has a delta of 0.5, then that implies that the option will increase by $0.50 for a $1.00 move up in the stock price. Conversely, if a put option has a delta of –0.5 that implies that the option will increase by $0.50 for a $1.00 move down in the stock price.

Generally speaking, ATM options have deltas of plus or minus 0.50, and deeper ITM options might have a delta of 0.80 or higher. Out-of-the-money options have deltas as small as 0.20 or less. These values will change as the option becomes further ITM or OTM. Option prices aren't linear, and neither are the changes in the option Greeks.

Applying delta

When an option is very deep ITM, it begins to trade like the stocks, moving practically dollar-for-dollar with the underlying stock. In contrast, far OTM options won't move much at all, even if the stock price starts rising or falling.

Steer clear of buying options that are far OTM. Your chances of making money buying short-term OTM options are generally pretty small because the option's premium rapidly deteriorates. You also need a large move in the right direction from the underlying stock price in order to become profitable.

The delta of an option can also be thought of as an option's chance of being in-the-money by expiration. It represents the statistical probability of an option finishing in-the-money at expiration. For example, if a call has a delta of 0.35, you have, in theory, a 35% chance of the call finishing in-the-money at expiration.

Calculating delta

Successful option traders usually are proficient at understanding and calculating deltas. Several tools on the market can automatically calculate an option's delta, but you can also calculate deltas manually by using the following formula:

$$(\text{Option's Price Change}) \div (\text{Stock's Price Change}) = \text{Delta}$$

For example, assume XYZ is trading at $15 per share and you buy an ATM 15 call option. If the call option increases $0.20 in price while XYZ increases $0.40 per share, the delta would then be:

$$0.2/0.4 = 0.50$$

In trading, this is a 50 delta, which means that this particular option will move at 50% of the speed of the stock price.

Computer models can be used to calculate delta with other variables involved, but for on-the-run calculations, use this formula to get a sense of delta.

A change in the stock price causes a change in the option delta, which causes a change in the overall position delta.

Gamma

Gamma is the rate of change in the delta for each one-point move in the underlying instrument. It tells you the degree by which the delta changes in relation to changes in the underlying instrument's price.

The gamma helps you forecast changes in the delta of an option or an overall position.

For example, a call option with a gamma of 0.03 indicates that the option will gain 0.03 positive deltas for each point increase in the stock price. A put option with a gamma of 0.03 indicates that the option will gain 0.03 negative deltas for each point decrease in the stock price.

Gamma is especially useful when larger positions are in place. It provides a more dynamic risk profile of the option position. Gamma is highest for ATM options because the deltas of ATM options are more sensitive to price moves in the underlying stock.

Theta

Theta is a measure of the time decay of an option; it reflects the change in the price of an option as it moves closer to expiration. Theta measures the amount an option will lose with the passage of one day.

Generally speaking, theta increases as an option approaches expiration. Theta is one of the most important concepts for a beginning option trader to understand. It basically explains the effect of time on the premium of the options that have been purchased or sold. The less time that an option has until expiration, the faster that option is going to lose its extrinsic value (see Chapter 4).

Theta measures the rate at which value is lost. The further out in time you go, the smaller the time decay for an option. Therefore, if you want to own an option, purchasing longer-term contracts is a good idea. If you're using a strategy that profits from time decay, then you will want to be short (sell) the shorter-term options to take advantage of the loss in value due to time decay (which can happen quickly).

Vega

Vega is the change in the price of an option with respect to its change in volatility. As the volatility of a stock increases, so does the premium for its options.

Volatility is one of the most important determinants of an option's price. (Chapter 5 tells you more about volatility.) The easiest way to understand volatility is to view a price chart over a period of time and look at the price change; the greater the price change, the higher the volatility. Vega measures the amount an option will gain or lose with a one-percentage point change in volatility.

Determining Risk with the Greeks

The Greeks can help you to explore the various risk exposures of every trade you consider placing. Options have a variety of risk exposures and these risks can vary dramatically with time and market movement. To recognize the probabilities of the trade making money, you have to be able to determine a variety of risk exposure measurements. Changes in the price of the underlying instrument trigger changes in the delta, which triggers changes in all of the Greeks.

The option Greeks are available as part of the theoretical option price calculator on the CBOE Web site. Take time to study the effects that changes in price, time and volatility have on the Greeks and how they interrelate.

You don't have to understand all the mathematics behind the Greeks, but you do need to know how to interpret the numbers and how these numbers measure how an option or option strategy will behave given certain changes in market conditions. Because prices are constantly changing, the Greeks provide traders with the means to determine just how sensitive a specific trade is to price fluctuations.

The best way to calculate the Greeks is by using option analysis software such as Optionetics Platinum (www. optionetics.com/platinum.)

Chapter 7

Making Trades, Mitigating Stress

*Y*ou've narrowed down the type of trade you're going to place, chosen the appropriate asset to utilize, and exhaustively researched the right entry and exit prices. Now what? You've got to correctly place your trade or all that work may go for naught. This chapter gives you a look at some of the ways the process might pan out, and how you can make your investing experience as pleasant as possible.

The Trading Process: Stocks versus Options

Although technology has made the process of placing trades into the market last but a few seconds, you still find an extensive number of processes involved in the execution of a trade.

An order begins when a trader contacts his broker. From there, the order goes through a series of steps on its way to execution. The process that the order goes through depends on your broker, the instrument being traded, and the type of order you're placing.

You work with a broker to trade stocks and options in much the same way. The upcoming sections give you a rundown of the process for each.

Buying and selling stocks

The following steps outline the process of buying and selling stocks in the U.S. markets:

1. **Place an order with your broker by phone or online to buy or sell a certain number of shares.**

2. **Your broker enters the order into his trading system.**

   If you enter the order online, depending upon the broker's setup, the order may be sent directly to the appropriate exchange.

3. **Brokers and exchange systems match buy and sell orders and trade them automatically.**

   Best-priced orders have priority. If there's more than one order at the same price, the order that was placed first takes precedence. Large orders have no priority over small orders.

4. **The trade occurs when the buy and sell orders are matched.**

   Your broker may notify you by phone or e-mail to confirm that your order has been filled. You can easily check your order confirmation online.

Buying and selling options

The following steps outline the process of buying and selling options in the U.S. markets:

1. **Place an order with your broker by phone or online to buy or sell a certain number of options contracts.**

   You may be buying or selling to open a trade, or buying or selling to close a trade.

2. **Your broker enters the order into her trading system.**

If you enter the order online, depending upon the broker's setup, the order may be sent directly to the appropriate exchange.

3. The order is executed on the exchange by a price and time priority basis.

The order is generally routed automatically to one of six options exchanges. A trade is executed when the order price satisfies current market conditions, assuming there is sufficient interest on the bid or offer to meet the size of your order. If your order is outside of the current market (too low when buying or too high when selling), it's placed in a queue until it better aligns with the market.

4. The trade occurs when the buy and sell orders are matched.

The broker may notify you by phone or email to confirm that your order has been filled. The order confirmation may be easily checked online.

Structural Changes in the U.S. options market

In recent years, options trading has become easier than it used to be. Two historic structural changes (linkage and price improvement) in the way the options market operates in the United States have resulted in a market environment that's extremely execution-friendly for option traders.

In 2003, the five options markets (AMEX, CBOE, ISE, PHLX, and PCX) underwent significant structural changes when the Intermarket Linkage Program was completed. The United States no longer had five disjointed option markets; connectivity among the exchanges made it easier for all exchanges to either execute an order at the National Best Bid and Offer (NBBO) or to send the order to the exchange that was posting the NBBO. Although certain conditions may prevent an order from being executed at the NBBO, intermarket linkage of the option exchanges in the United States has provided a means for all orders to access the NBBO.

In 2004, when the Boston Options Exchange (BOX) began trading, it also participated in the linkage program. The BOX also added another new dimension for option trading — the introduction of price improvement below the normal $0.05 or $0.10 spreads. Now option execution can occur at $0.01 increments for price-improved orders.

Looking At Types of Options Orders

The type of order that you use to place an option trade is a very important part of the ordering process. Which one you choose depends on your style of trading. A long-term trader is generally happy with a limit order, or he or she may be happy with a market order in a liquid but stable market. In contrast, a short-term trader probably uses a wide range of order types, including conditional orders such as stop loss. A market order is the most popular type of order, followed by the limit order.

Market orders

A *market order* means that you're willing to pay the lowest asking price, or sell at the highest offer price, at the time your order is submitted. That price may or may not be the price quoted! Markets move quickly and someone may have entered a huge buy order two seconds before yours hits the market, nudging the best ask price up a few cents just before your order arrives.

Limit orders

A *limit order* indicates that you're willing to pay the price you choose (or less), or sell at the price you choose (or more).

If you say, "I'm buying to open 10 October DELL 35 call contracts at a limit of $1.00," then you have entered a limit order that requires your broker to purchase the 10 DELL call contracts at $1.00 each ($100 per contract) or less.

Advanced strategies

Combination orders are generally used with advanced strategies to create a position to capitalize on current market conditions and your outlook for the future. Two combination positions serve as the base for a variety of other strategies: the spread and the straddle. The glossary explains each strategy.

Limit orders guarantee the price you want, or they don't get filled. Plain and simple. Why is this so important? Well, in an equity trade, if you place a market order and wind up paying an extra quarter point on a $75 stock, that's a relatively insignificant 1/3 of 1 percent. If you pay a quarter point more on a $4 call option, that's over 6 percent. Because the cost of options is lower, the extra 1/4 point is a much higher percentage of the total.

To maximize your profit potential, use limit orders whenever possible!

Combination orders

A combination order is an order containing two or more options with different strikes or expiration dates. Most advanced option strategies require you to use a combination order. Such orders require additional attention to detail so that they are placed correctly.

When you place a combination option order, you need to instruct your broker to execute the orders "simultaneously" to make sure they happen together. You want to avoid *legging-in* one side at a time. Legging-in increases the risk of not being able to fill both sides of your position, thereby ending up with only half of the trade placed.

When you place a combination trade as a limit order, it goes to the market with a net price that you want to pay or receive for the combination. It's the broker's responsibility to match up the options, complete the transaction, and deliver the final trade to your account. Don't panic if the individual (leg) option prices vary; as long as the net debit or credit for the combination is within your net limits, your profitability doesn't change.

By placing both sides of the position simultaneously, you will likely have an easier time monitoring and analyzing your trade as you go along. If you're new to combination option strategies, always follow the rule of opening and closing the entire position at the same time, rather than individually.

Placing an Order Effectively

Learning to place an order correctly is vital to becoming a good trader. Each time you find an optimal trade, you need to write down the whole order exactly as you're going to place it with your broker. Brokers always tape-record orders, so there is no room for mistakes.

If you make a mistake when you place a trade, you are nonetheless required to go through with the trade, regardless of the outcome.

If you use an online broker, make sure you have a thorough understanding of the site's order-placing procedures. For example, some online brokers can't handle spread orders online. You may still have to call your broker and place them verbally.

Bullish call: An example order

So you're bullish on XYZ and want to purchase an in-the-money call option that will expire in three months. Here's how you do it:

> I'd like to buy to open 2 XYZ March 30 calls at a limit price of $1.00 good for the day.

Don't hesitate to tell your broker you're new to option trading. She really is there to help you get comfortable.

Assuming XYZ moved upward, later you can exit the position with the following order:

> I want to sell to close 2 XYZ March 30 calls at a limit price of $1.40 good for the day.

Online orders usually incorporate some kind of two-step process. Even with built-in protections, it's still possible to go long when you mean to go short, and short when you mean to go long. You need to be as careful as you can.

Terminology is also an important part of placing the order. When you enter an order to create a new option position in your account, you're using an *opening* order. When you exit an existing option position, you're using a *closing* order. Refer to Chapter 2 for the proper way to define the options you wish to trade.

The following are the four most common order actions for entering and exiting option positions:

- ✔ **Buy to open:** Used when entering new long call or long put (or a combination) position.

- ✔ **Sell to open:** Used when entering new short call or short put (or a combination) position.

- ✔ **Sell to close:** Used when exiting an existing long call or long put (or a combination) position. You must be holding the position long in your account if you plan to sell to close.

- ✔ **Buy to close:** Used when exiting an existing short call or short put (or a combination) position. You must be holding the position short in your account if you want to buy to close.

Always double check your orders. Although many traders may believe that placing a trade is the easy part, in actual fact, placing an order is quite complex. Mistakes are easy to make and can be very expensive.

Curtailing Stress

Risk is directly tied to an investor's worst enemy: stress. When you're stressed out, your decision-making skills are not at their best, and that's a recipe for disaster when it comes to trading. It's a vicious cycle: Experience stress, make bad decisions, lose capital, get more stressed. Keep your stress level low by minimizing your losses.

Optionetics ensures your survival as a trader by reducing the stress usually associated with trading. Optionetics strategies maximize profits and minimize loss by using options to protect existing positions and hedge risk. But reducing stress is only the beginning. As a trader, you also need to develop patience, perseverance, and a willingness to try the unorthodox. In other words, trading is a craft that must be developed. It combines instinct with analysis, courage with humility, and chance with intention. It can be exciting or devastating depending on your point of view. Many roads lead to one destination: making money in the markets.

Because reducing stress is essential to making money in the markets, you need to create a low-stress master investment plan. Try taking the following steps:

1. Quantify your risk.
2. Develop a flexible investment plan.
3. Build your knowledge base systematically.
4. Acquire and use your trading tools.
5. Pinpoint your risk tolerance.
6. Apply trade sizing principles.
7. Find a good options broker.

The following sections explain exactly how to go about these stress-reducing principles in more detail.

Quantify your risk

You've no doubt heard that old proverb "cut your losses and let your profits run." Traders can make large profits by placing the right trade at the right time. Each trade has a corresponding risk. No secret there.

Predetermine the risk in the trade

By using Optionetics strategies, a trader can predefine the risk and reward of each trade to determine how likely it is to pay off. If you decide that the risk is worth it and that you can afford the potential loss, then you can calmly place the trade.

When you thoroughly analyze a trade before placing it, you know your maximum risk and potential reward. By placing only trades that suit your personal risk tolerance, your stress level naturally decreases.

Predetermine the risk to your account

You absolutely must assess the level of risk you can afford to take before placing your first trade. Placing trades that are too large relative to the size of your account or letting your losses build puts you at a risk of ruin. That means literally that your funds will run out.

Pinpointing your risk means you identify both numeric risk that makes sense for your account size as well as the risk that allows you to sleep at night.

Before you invest a single dollar, you need to make an honest appraisal of your financial assets and capabilities. Consider factors such as these:

- ✔ How much disposable income do you earn monthly?
- ✔ How much money do you need to set aside for life's little (and big) emergencies?
- ✔ How much of your savings can you afford to lose?

You can buy real estate with no money down, but you need cash to open a brokerage account. When you put up cash to invest in stocks, you are coming face-to-face with risk. Hopefully, you'll never lose your entire trading account, but you need to be prepared in the event that you do.

Develop a flexible investment plan

When your investment plan is flexible, you have a range of strategies that allow you to take advantage of a variety of market situations. This approach means you don't over-leverage your account and are able to establish new positions when the market changes directions. You have exit points that suit your risk and are executed with stop loss orders to avoid emotional decision-making. A flexible plan doesn't require you to monitor the market minute by minute.

Option traders have built-in agility because they can benefit from market movement in either direction. Assuming a bull market is in progress, but appears to be weakening, the option trader can begin to exit profitable bullish positions while also adding small bearish positions in weaker groups.

Without a flexible plan and solid tools, traders have to rely on hunches when it comes to forecasting where the market appears to be going. One way to organize your strategies is to list them with the market conditions in which they're best used. Such conditions include, bullish, bearish, or neutral for direction and high or low for volatility.

Investors and traders have to be entrepreneurial by nature. One of the greatest attributes an entrepreneur in any industry can develop is the ability to change directions when a roadblock appears. Traders need to exhibit this flexibility if they are to survive in the marketplace.

Build your knowledge base systematically

Most traders begin with simplistic strategies such as going long or going short the market. (See Chapter 1.) Maybe they use stops versus limit or market orders. Some just listen to their brokers and follow their trading ideas.

Starting slowly with basic strategies doesn't pose a problem; it's when you stop there that you limit your chances for success. If trading were simply a matter of placing a couple of orders and walking away, everyone would be doing it. It's a challenge that requires continual study and development.

By starting with strategies that suit market conditions and that you readily grasp, you build good trading habits such as doing your homework and taking losses. This allows you to stay in the game long enough to participate in changing markets and develop new strategies that work accordingly.

Traders who learn to specialize in one area at a time are at a definite advantage. Specialization enables them to become thoroughly educated on what kinds of market conditions are necessary for a strategy to make money.

Acquire and use your trading tools

The fourth key step in managing and reducing stress is selecting and efficiently using trading tools.

Keep in mind that trading is a business, even if it's something you do on a very small scale when you come home from your "regular job." This attitude means you need to dedicate two precious resources to the venture: time and money.

Your investment in time entails formal learning through books and courses, creating a plan, developing your skills by paper trading and starting small, re-assessing your plan, and doing your homework on the markets every day that your plan requires.

The investment of money includes the cost of books and courses, small initial losses you should expect as a new trader, and tools to help you assess the market and select the appropriate trades. Such tools may be a subscription to a business paper, magazine, or educational newsletter (not a "hot pick" newsletter); analysis software; or continuing education as your trading style dictates.

Optionetics offers a variety of trading tools, which you can find out about at www.optionetics.com.

Apply trade sizing principles

There are a variety of approaches to *trade sizing* — the systematic approach to determining the number of shares or contracts purchased based on a specific maximum position value. By establishing rational rules for trade sizing, the trader has a plan that allows him/her to be wrong on a trade without severe consequences. Because sometimes a wrong decision is simply part of trading, it's good to have a plan that takes it into account.

Basic approaches to trade sizing include identifying a fixed maximum dollar amount per trade or a percentage of assets.

Using a fixed per-trade maximum

Delineating a maximum per-trade value means that you determine before you enter any trade a maximum dollar amount allowed for each trade as part of an overall trade approach. By planning this out way before you evaluate any single trade, you prevent yourself from "betting the farm" on what feels like a great trade. The maximum dollar amount is a fixed number that you don't exceed no matter how good a trade may look before you execute it.

The downside of using a fixed dollar amount is that this approach doesn't consider fluctuations in your trading account. (That's why the next section discusses using a fixed maximum percentage of your trading account as an alternate approach.)

In terms of the fixed dollar amount, for example, a $1,000 maximum trade allocation represents a greater portion of your account value when you encounter a losing run, because the account value is declining. This $1,000 may start to represent too large a percentage of the account.

When you are growing your account, a fixed value represents a smaller percentage allocation. Now, your trade allocations may be artificially low as you achieve more trading success, which leads to an increasing account size. This fluctuation doesn't happen when you set a fixed percentage value.

Although a fixed maximum trade size is better than no trading rule for this critical decision, traders generally don't want to increase allocations when they're out of step with the markets (losing run).

Trading a percentage of your assets

Another approach is to trade using only a fixed percentage of your assets. Identify a percentage of your total investment assets (such as 70 percent) that you allocate to meet your future needs, and then ear-mark the remaining portion for trading. Although you may move surplus trading dollars back into your investments, never move money allocated to your future needs to make up for a trading short-fall. You need to re-accumulate savings for trading, if appropriate.

Given a certain trading account allocation, you can use a fixed percentage value of the cash available in the account as your maximum trade amount. Because the amount of cash in the trading account varies over time, the amount you allocate to each trade varies as well. Set a reasonable initial fixed percentage and work with it for 3 to 6 months. If you think that the account is declining too quickly, reduce the fixed percentage and if you think that the trade values are too small (and your account is rising slowly), increase the fixed percentage.

After an initial adjustment period, you need to periodically (at least annually) re-evaluate your trade allocations. At this time, you can also shift assets from a growing trading account into a longer-term investment account, as appropriate.

The advantage of this system is that it takes into consideration changing account values. When you use a fixed dollar amount (as explained in the preceding section), the corresponding percent allocation per trade rises after a string of losses. In contrast, a percentage allocation for trade sizing provides flexibility for varying account values and prevents an account from going bust.

Now a trader definitely needs to step back if the account is declining to that extent, but from a mathematical standpoint, a percent allocation can technically only approach zero.

Theory aside, percent allocations also enable the trader to easily incorporate strategy allocations (for example, high volatility, contrarian, and so on) into the mix.

Find a good options broker

Choosing a broker is one of the most important decisions you'll ever make. Your broker is, in effect, your trading partner. Her response time is critical to attaining the best trading results.

Options traders and non-options traders can choose from many types of brokers. After you fully understand the risks and characteristics of listed options, look into the types of brokers and determine what you need.

A broker needs to provide a trader the following:

- ✔ A user-friendly platform with uncomplicated option order entry screens
- ✔ Reliable, high-quality executions
- ✔ Options data and analysis tools
- ✔ Reasonable commissions

Check out the broker review section of the Optionetics Web site, www.optionetics.com.

Part III
Part of Tens

The 5th Wave   By Rich Tennant

"You bought options on what? You know we're on a budget. Now take Hughes Electric back to General Motors and see if you can get your money back."

In this part . . .

*I*n true Dummies tradition, this part offers you handy "top ten" lists for quick reference on two critical issues: what you need to ask your broker before you make your first options trade and how to make the most of all the cool tools and information Optionetics has to offer online and through other helpful resources.

Chapter 8

Ten Questions to Ask Your Broker

*T*o trade options, you need to set up an equity options account with a brokerage institution. Generally, brokers fall into four basic categories:

- ✔ **Full-service brokers** have higher commissions because they research the markets in order to provide value-added services, such as investment advice, to clients.

- ✔ **Discount brokers** offer reduced commissions and stripped-down services that typically include placing orders and facilitating exits.

- ✔ **Deep-discount brokers** offer more attractive commission rates than full-service or discount brokers, but primarily trade large blocks for investors with large sums.

- ✔ **Specialized options brokers** provide specialized expertise to the rapidly growing options trading community and most offer low commission rates.

Choosing the Right Broker for You

When evaluating brokers, limit yourself to those with a trading philosophy that matches yours. For best results, choose a brokerage that specializes in options trading for both beginners and advanced traders.

Your main objective is selecting a broker who is best able to execute your transactions according to your wishes — and at the lowest price possible. In particular, you want an experienced, unbiased broker with in-depth knowledge about options trading.

 Remember that brokers are paid commissions when you place your trades, regardless of whether the trades actually make any money. The commission fee varies depending on what kind of service your broker provides. Be sure to compare rates and fees before committing yourself to any broker.

Top Ten Questions to Ask a Prospective Broker

Following are some key questions to ask any broker you are considering trading through:

✔ What options-related educational resources and trading tools do you offer?

✔ Can your online service execute complex options orders such as spreads, straddles, and combination strategies in one trade online?

✔ What is your minimum account size for options trading, and what margin requirements do you demand?

✔ How fast are orders executed?

✔ What is your commission fee schedule? Are there hidden fees that I should be aware of?

✔ Do you offer trading via telephone and online trading via Internet/computer?

✓ Can I trade after hours?

✓ Do you offer streaming real-time quotes?

✓ Do you provide stock charts, earnings estimates, research reports, screening, alerts, quotes, and news on your Web site?

✓ Do you offer a trading demo that lets you develop hypothetical trades and view the results?

Checking options after market hours

Be sure you find a broker who can accept orders after market hours so that the orders are filled the moment the market opens on the following day. One of the benefits of trading options is that you can manage your positions in your spare time, in the evenings, or on weekends when the markets are closed. In fact, you do not need to have access to the markets during the day to trade. What's more, many professional options traders recommend not trading during market hours in order to avoid making impulsive moves.

Chapter 9

Ten Ways to Get More from Optionetics

*O*ptionetics is to trading what the scientific method is to biology. It's a systematic approach to option trading that focuses on reducing risk first in order to profit from the financial markets. It encompasses self-assessment; a trading plan; market, stock, and option analysis; and trade management to implement low-risk, high-reward strategies.

Optionetics gives you the information you need to become a successful options trader. Of course, none of that matters if you don't put it to use. Here are a few ways you can find out about Optionetics techniques.

Walk through the Web Site

At www.optionetics.com, you find all of the resources you need to make your trading easier — and more profitable. From basic options terminology to advanced concepts to sophisticated trading strategies, you're sure to benefit by the comprehensive yet easy-to-understand explanations.

The Web site also features in-depth descriptions about Optionetics seminars, workshops, at-home study programs, books, publications, home study materials, trading tools, software, and other product offerings. You can also check class schedules and availability, and register online.

What's more, the Web site contains loads of useful tools for:

- Selecting a brokerage
- Accessing and managing your Optionetics Platinum trading account
- Researching the markets and analyzing trade opportunities
- Looking up stock and options quotes, volatility rankings, and more
- Chatting with fellow traders and exchanging trading ideas via Optionetics discussion boards
- Perusing online trading articles (dozens of new articles per week!) written exclusively for www.Optionetics.com by professional traders and industry experts.

As a trader, you can quickly set up an account on My Optionetics, which provides quick and easy access to your favorite www.Optionetics.com information. As a registered member of My Optionetics, you can create a fully customizable, personalized page filled with features such as:

- Charts of the major stock indices
- The latest market commentary
- Schedules of upcoming seminars and events in your area
- Links to Optionetics publications

You can also manage your Optionetics personal profile, set up online stock portfolios, and access your preferred Optionetics discussion boards — all from a single location.

With an unmatched breadth and depth of education and trading resources, www.Optionetics.com is a great way to become the successful trader you've always wanted to be.

Master new high-reward, low-risk strategies, brush up on your trading skills and optimize your earnings potential. It all starts with Optionetics.

Attend Trading Seminars and Workshops

Optionetics' wide variety of classes provides traders of all levels the chance to refine their trading skills and explore new wealth-building strategies. Packed with plenty of trading demonstrations, case studies, Q&A discussions, and more, its offerings range from the flagship two-day Optionetics Seminar to advanced and masters-level courses to interactive computer-based learning opportunities, and even a floating seminar aboard a Caribbean cruise liner. Optionetics also offers home-based learning opportunities, mentoring, and more.

Instructors are all professional traders who have "walked the walk" down Wall Street and understand market dynamics. They trade using the same high-profit, low-risk, low-stress strategies that they teach at the seminars, giving students a unique insider perspective into the rewarding world of options.

Peruse Trading Publications

Informative trading newsletters offer invaluable opportunities to stay current on market trends. Optionetics publications provide added value by including case studies and trade ideas in each issue, along with educational articles and other topical market data. Readers can track trade examples from issue to issue to gauge their progress and better understand trade dynamics.

Most Optionetics subscription-based publications are niche-oriented toward specific trading strategies, enabling traders to focus on the kinds of trades they prefer most. Depending on the publication, they are available biweekly, weekly, or monthly, and are conveniently accessible online.

Study at Home

Workbooks, study guides, videos, books, CDs, and DVDs help traders of all levels to practice and strengthen their skills from the comfort of home. With no schedules to clear, no driving time, and no required time commitment, you can learn virtually whenever you want at your own pace.

What's more, Optionetics' at-home study is completely customizable, enabling you to focus on your favorite strategies and skip over techniques that don't suit your particular trading style. Optionetics' home study materials also include challenging exercises and quizzes so you can make sure you have the concepts down before you apply real money to the markets.

Draw on Trading Software

You need the right tools to be a successful trader. Software applications (with paper trading capabilities) help you accomplish a number of tasks, saving you time and effort while producing better results.

With Optionetics software, you can

- ✓ Identify opportunities.

- ✓ Isolate appropriate trade candidates.

- ✓ Manage your trades through execution.

- ✓ Perform technical and fundamental analysis before you enter trades.

Many software packages integrate seamlessly for easy data transfer, compounding the value of the individual applications and enabling traders to accomplish even more.

Take Part in the Super-Summit

Featuring top traders, instructors, and world-class entertainment, the Optionetics Annual Super-Investor Summit (OASIS) held every June packs three days of education and excitement into one incredible trading summit. From the kick-off Welcome Reception to the Optionetics Comedy Club on Saturday night (past headliners include Jay Leno, Bill Cosby, and Kevin James), OASIS is a trader's ultimate destination.

This incredible educational event includes dozens of breakout sessions on topics not offered at Optionetics seminars, giving you the chance to learn a wealth of new information and enhance your skills. OASIS also features software demos, panel discussions, guest speakers, great food, A-list entertainment, and much more.

Thousands of Optionetics traders around the world come to OASIS each year to learn, share trading stories, strategize, and network person-to-person. In fact, many friendships built around Optionetics discussion boards come to fruition at OASIS.

Talk with Other Traders

Interaction with a local or global options trading community is a great way to exchange ideas, discuss trading tactics, and gain new insight.

With a variety of Optionetics discussion boards available, you can select forums based on specific strategies, skill level (beginner through advanced), geographic location, and many additional criteria. Another valuable benefit of joining discussion boards is the opportunity to post questions to trading experts and Optionetics instructors, who are all happy to share their knowledge with budding traders eager to learn more. In fact, many Optionetics classes include exclusive discussion boards, giving students a chance to communicate directly with their classmates and teachers.

Follow Market Commentary

Successful traders understand that staying abreast of market activities and economic data, as well as having a good general sense of what's going on in the world, can have a significant impact on their winnings.

The Optionetics Web site offers a unique opportunity for you to get inside the heads of professional traders and find out what they recommend, what they avoid, and how they grow their money during varying market conditions. Every day, Optionetics posts dozens of articles written by industry insiders and professional traders exclusively for www. optionetics.com. The commentary is topical, insightful, and offers new viewpoints for traders in the midst of planning their next moves.

Get the Scoop on Brokers

Brokers come in all shapes and sizes, and what works for one trader may not work for another. Many traders just starting out may benefit by the hand-holding expertise that full-service brokerages provide, whereas seasoned traders may prefer a no-frills brokerage with an eye on deep discounts.

You are always encouraged to do your own homework before signing on with any broker. The Optionetics Web site provides an extensive comparison chart that ranks many of today's most popular brokerages and offers practical tips and insight for traders in search of the perfect broker.

Discover Wealth Preservation Education

Making money is only half of the story; the other often-neglected half involves the ability for individuals to keep more of their earnings, and that requires careful planning.

Wealth preservation seminars from Optionetics not only cover the basics (asset protection and tax-saving strategies), but also provide valuable information for sophisticated traders who are considering setting up a trading business entity or who are using their trading as a full-time business. The information in these seminars is also useful if you have established a corporate entity and want to explore ways of better managing it for optimal tax benefits.

Rest Easy — Everything's Guaranteed

Optionetics stands by its pledge to provide traders of all levels with high-profit, limited-risk trade strategy education. That's why many of our seminars and products are backed by our full money-back guarantee.

Appendix

A Trader's Glossary

Ask: An indication by a trader or a dealer of a willingness to sell a security or a commodity; the price at which an investor can buy from a broker-dealer.

Assignment: When the short option position is notified of the long position's intent to exercise. When assigned, the short contract holder must meet the obligation. A short call requires delivery of shares whereas a short put requires purchasing shares.

At-the-money (ATM): An option is at-the-money when its strike price is equal to the current share price of its underlying security.

Bear market: A falling stock market over a prolonged period of time, usually caused by a weak economy and decreasing profits. A bear market usually lasts at least six months and no more than eighteen months.

Bear Put Spread: A *vertical spread* that creates a debit in the account and is established by purchasing a higher strike put and selling a lower strike put with the same expiration dates. The bear put strategy has both limited profit potential and limited downside risk.

Bid: The highest price a prospective buyer is prepared to pay for a specified time for a trading unit of a specified security.

Bond: A debt obligation issued by a government (such as a Treasury bond) or corporation (such as a corporate bond) that promises to pay its bondholders periodic interest at a fixed rate (the coupon), and to repay the principal of the loan at maturity (a specified future date).

Breakdown: A stock move below a major price support area that paves the way for continued downward movement. *See also* **Support.**

Breakeven: The point where the option trader has covered all of the costs of the strategy.

Breakout: The stock move above a major resistance level or below a major support level. *See also* **Resistance.**

Bull Call Spread: A *vertical spread* that creates a debit in the account and is established by purchasing a lower strike call and selling a higher strike call with the same expiration dates. The bull call strategy has both limited profit potential and limited downside risk.

Bull market: A rising stock market over a prolonged period of time, usually caused by a strong economy and subsequent increased profits.

Calendar Spread: A strategy that can be used when a gradual trend or sideways move in the underlying security is expected. It is sometimes called a *horizontal spread* or *time spread* because it uses two options with the same strike price but different expiration dates. In most cases, the option strategist creates a calendar spread by purchasing a longer-term option and selling a short-term option.

Call option: An option contract that gives the holder the right, but not the obligation, to buy a specified amount of an underlying security at a specified price within a specified time.

Class: All of the options for one underlying security of the same type (put or call). For example, GE put options are a class of options.

Collateral: Any form of security accepted by OCC to offset margin obligations. This can include shares, cash, bank guarantees, or shares bought on margin

Cover: A stock transaction that closes an existing position. It is commonly used when exiting a short position (as in, "cover the short stock").

Credit: Funds brought into a brokerage account from the sale of an option. It can be as a result of off-setting an existing long position, the short sale of a new single option position, or the completion of a combination position that nets funds.

Debit: Funds used from a brokerage account for the purchase of an option. It can be as a result of purchasing a new long position, off-setting an existing short position, or the completion of a combination position that requires funds.

Delta: The ratio of change in the price of a derivative with the price of the underlying asset.

Derivative: A security, such as an option contract, whose value is determined in part from the value of another security referred to as the underlying security.

Equity option: An option with a stock serving as the underlying security.

Ex-dividend: Without dividend. Due to the timing of the transaction, the buyer of stock will not own the stock on the declared record date and will not receive a pending dividend.

Execute: Execute refers to the completion of a trade.

Exercise: A call option is exercised when the buyer takes delivery of the underling asset at the option's strike price. A put option is exercised when the buyer sells the underlying asset at the option's strike price.

Expiration date: The last day for American-style options may be exercised; the only day European- style options may be exercised. For stock options, this date is the Saturday immediately following the 3rd Friday of the expiration month.

Fill: An executed order; sometimes refers to the price at which an order is executed.

Front month: The first expiration month for an option in a series of months.

Futures: Contracts covering the purchase and sale of financial instruments or physical commodities for future delivery on a commodity futures exchange.

Gamma: The rate of change for delta with respect to the underlying asset's price.

Gap: A day in which the daily range is completely above or below the previous day's daily range.

Going long: To buy stock, options, or futures in order to profit from a rise in the market price.

Going short: Selling a security that is not owned, thereby creating a short position.

Greeks: A group of theoretical values that determine how specific market changes will affect the price of an option. Greeks include delta, gamma, theta, and vega.

Hedge: To create a trade that lowers the risk of a strong move in either direction; an investment made to reduce the risk of adverse price movements in a security.

HOLDRS: Acronym for Holding Company Depository Receipts, which are exchange-traded funds that hold baskets of stocks from specific industry groups.

Implied volatility (IV): A measure of an underlying stock's expected volatility as reflected in an option's price.

Index: A group of stocks that make up a portfolio in which performance can be monitored based upon one calculation.

In-the-money (ITM): A call option is in-the-money when the strike price is below the current share price. A put option is in-the-money when the strike price is above the current share price.

Intrinsic value: The portion of an option's price that is not affected by time decay; the amount by which the strike price is in-the-money.

Leg-into: Trading one part (leg) of a strategy and then trading the other leg at a later date. This is an alternative to establishing the strategy as a single trade; however, consideration needs to be made to ensure that strategy will still be effective if it is taken in two separate steps.

Liquidity: A measure of availability of a security; the ease in which a stock can be bought or sold at current prices; closely associated with volume.

Limit order: An order to buy a stock at or below a specified price or to sell a stock at or above a specified price.

Long: An ownership position in a stock, option, or other investment. Being long is generally considered a bullish strategy that profits when the price of the asset moves higher.

Margin: A security payment (in the form of cash or any other acceptable cover) made to the OCC to ensure that an investor's obligations are met.

Market order: Buying or selling securities at the price given at the time the order reaches the exchange.

Moneyness: An option characteristics that describes the current price of the underlying relative to the option strike price and type.

Naked option: A call or put option written (sold) without a hedge position.

NBBO (National Best Bid-Offer): The most advantageous market for buyers and sellers given all bids and asking prices on all exchanges trading the security.

Offset: A method of exiting a trade by reversing the original transaction. If you sell a call, you offset this by buying a call with the same strike price and expiration.

Options Clearing Corporation (OCC): The entity responsible for clearing U.S. option trades and managing option account margin balances as well as exercise and assignment transactions for the option markets.

Out-of-the-money (OTM): A call option is out-of-the-money when the strike price is above the current share price. A put option is out-of-the-money when the strike price is below the current share price.

Put option: An option contract that gives the buyer the right, but not the obligation, to sell a specified amount of an underlying security at a specified price within a specified time.

Premium: The price paid to purchase a call or put option or received as a credit for selling a call or put option.

Price improvement: An action taken by exchange market makers and specialists to provide a trade execution that is better than the existing market (Bid or Ask).

Resistance: A term used in technical analysis to identify a price area in which a security has difficulty exceeding. It can be considered a temporary ceiling on prices where selling pressure enters the market.

Rho: The rate at which the price of a derivative changes with interest rates.

Risk-free rate of return: The interest rate associated with 90-day U.S. Treasury Bills which are guaranteed by the full faith and taxing authority of the federal government. These securities are deemed without risk and therefore serve as the basis for comparing returns from securities that are not guaranteed.

Rolling down: Closing a current option and opening one with a lower strike price.

Rolling forward: Closing a current option and opening one with a longer term to expiration; also called *rolling out.*

Rolling up: Closing a current option and buying one with a higher strike price.

Series: All of the options of one class with the same strike price and expiration date.

Short: Generally a bearish position that profits from a move lower in the stock or option. A short seller borrows shares from the broker and sells them at the current market price. The shares are eventually bought back and returned to the broker. Investors can also short puts and calls which are not borrowed, but rather created by the OCC. A short instrument is one that has been sold by the trader. A sold put option is a short option.

Short Selling: The process of selling shares in the market by first borrowing those shares from their broker. When initiating a position through a short sale, the trader must eventually purchase the shares in the market so they can be returned to the broker. Short selling essentially reverses the normal order of a stock transaction (buy to initiate the position, sell to close the position).

Spread order: *See Vertical Spread.*

Straddle: A combination position that consists of a call and a put with the same strike prices and expiration dates. The *long straddle* includes a long call and a long put, and is a limited risk, unlimited reward position that requires an explosive move in either direction to be profitable. The *short straddle* has unlimited risk and is not recommended.

Statistical volatility: A measure of a stock's propensity for movement based on the stock's past price action during a specific time period.

Stop Loss: A price level that triggers an alert or trade to minimize losses in a new position or prevent losses in a position that has unrealized gains. When a trader is long a position, the stop is below the current market for the security and when a trader is short a position, the stop is above the current market.

Strategy: A combination of long and short options and/or underlying securities used to limit risk and take advantage of market movement.

Strike price: Also called *exercise price,* the price at which the underlying security can be bought or sold if an option is exercised.

Support: A term used in technical analysis to identify a price area in which a security has difficulty dropping below. It can be considered a temporary floor on prices where buying demand enters the market.

Synthetic: An alternative combination of options and/or stock for a strategy that will produce the same risk and reward profile; a synthetic may provide a cheaper or more effective alternative under particular market conditions.

Technical Analysis: A form of security analysis that uses historical price and volume data to evaluate trends, cycles and supply/demand pressure through a variety of techniques.

Theta: Also referred to as *time decay*, theta is the change in an option price in relation to the decrease in time to expiration.

Time decay: A characteristic of option pricing, it is a reduction in value due to the passage of time.

Time value: Also referred to as *extrinsic value;* the difference between the option value and the intrinsic value. Extrinsic value decays over time.

Unwind: Unwinding a strategy is the reversal of the process used to enter the strategy.

Vega: The amount by which the price of an option changes when the volatility changes.

Vertical Spread: A trade that involves the simultaneous purchase and sale of options on the same stock with the same expiration date. The only difference between the options that are purchased and those that are sold is the strike price. Vertical spreads get their name from the image they create using an option table and can be created with puts or calls.

Volatility: A measure of an underlying security's expected price fluctuation over time. Essentially, the speed of market movement. Volatile stocks are more likely to move ITM or OTM before or at expiration than less-volatile stocks that move slowly.

Index

OPTIONETICS®
EMPOWERING INVESTORS

As a 2-day Optionetics® Seminar attendee, you'll also receive our complimentary Home Study Course prior to attending your scheduled seminar. It reinforces the innovative concepts, methods and trading techniques you'll see at this incredible educational event.

The complete package includes:

- TWO FULL DAYS of comprehensive instruction
- one Quick Start Guide
- four comprehensive manuals
- six DVDs
- 14 audio CDs

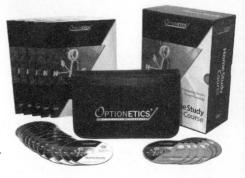

Plus, ALL seminar attendees receive a host of FREE BONUSES. Call for more details!

"[I made] $60,000+ profit.
I paid cash for a Lexus LS430."
– Warren B., Las Vegas, NV, Optionetics student since 2005

100% MONEY-BACK GUARANTEE

2 EASY WAYS TO RESERVE YOUR SEAT TODAY!

 Register online at www.dummies.optionetics.com.

 Call 888-284-3819 between 8 a.m. - 5 p.m. Pacific time, Monday-Friday.

Or visit us at:
www.dummies.optionetics.com